T0328447

Cambridge Elements ≡

Elements in Metaphysics
edited by
Tuomas E. Tahko
University of Bristol

RELATIONS

John Heil
Washington University in St. Louis, Monash University, Durham University

CAMBRIDGE
UNIVERSITY PRESS

CAMBRIDGE
UNIVERSITY PRESS

University Printing House, Cambridge CB2 8BS, United Kingdom

One Liberty Plaza, 20th Floor, New York, NY 10006, USA

477 Williamstown Road, Port Melbourne, VIC 3207, Australia

314–321, 3rd Floor, Plot 3, Splendor Forum, Jasola District Centre,
New Delhi – 110025, India

103 Penang Road, #05–06/07, Visioncrest Commercial, Singapore 238467

Cambridge University Press is part of the University of Cambridge.

It furthers the University's mission by disseminating knowledge in the pursuit of
education, learning, and research at the highest international levels of excellence.

www.cambridge.org
Information on this title: www.cambridge.org/9781108940610
DOI: 10.1017/9781108939904

© John Heil 2021

First published 2021

A catalogue record for this publication is available from the British Library.

ISBN 978-1-108-94061-0 Paperback
ISSN 2633-9862 (online)
ISSN 2633-9854 (print)

Relations

Elements in Metaphysics

DOI: 10.1017/9781108939904
First published online: October 2021

John Heil
Washington University in St. Louis, Monash University, Durham University

Author for correspondence: John Heil, john.heil@fulbrightmail.org

Abstract: Historically, philosophical discussions of relations have featured chiefly as afterthoughts, loose ends to be addressed only after coming to terms with more important and pressing metaphysical issues. F. H. Bradley stands out as an exception. Understanding Bradley's views on relations and their significance today requires an appreciation of the alternatives, which in turn requires an understanding of how relations have traditionally been classified and how philosophers have struggled to capture their nature and their ontological standing. Positions on these topics range from the rejection of relations altogether, to their being awarded the status as grounds for everything else, to various intermediary positions along this spectrum. Love them, hate them, or merely tolerate them, no philosopher engaged in ontologically serious metaphysics can afford to ignore relations.

Keywords: metaphysics, relations, truthmaking, supervenience, F. H. Bradley

ISBNs: 9781108940610 (PB), 9781108939904 (OC)
ISSNs: 2633-9862 (online), 2633-9854 (print)

Contents

1 Relations: Gotta Love 'Em

We inhabit a cosmos in which some things cause or bring about other things, some things are taller than others, some are warmer or heavier than others, a cosmos in which things stand at various distances from one another, in which things move from place to place, and in which you have a mother and a father and, maybe, a sibling or two – maybe you were a middle child. To describe our surroundings in this way is to describe relations among the objects that populate those surroundings.

At 1,149.4 m Ben Nevis is taller than 992 m Sgùrr Alasdair. Ben Nevis stands in the *taller than* relation to Sgùrr Alasdair. A regulation 160 g cricket ball is *heaver than* a 142 g baseball. San Francisco is 2,800 km *west* of St Louis. Elizabeth is the *sister of* Margaret and the *mother of* Anne. The italicised phrases express *relations*.

Talk of relations is indispensable, both in everyday life and in the sciences, but what exactly *are* relations? What makes it the case that relational judgements are true when they are true? Relational judgements aspire to objectivity. Relational judgements purport to be literally true. Relations and kinds of relation are plentiful. Why then do philosophers disagree so sharply over the nature of relations? Why do so many philosophers find relations enigmatic? Why do some go so far as to doubt the reality of relations? Is this just philosophers being philosophers, finding reasons to question what no sensible person would dream of questioning? Why must philosophers take something easy and turn it into something difficult?

With luck, these questions will answer themselves once you start thinking seriously about the nature of relations. Doing so requires a foray into metaphysics and, in particular, that branch of metaphysics philosophers call ontology. Ontology concerns what there is, not in the sense of compiling lists of individual entities as you might list the contents of your medicine cabinet, but in the sense of working out the most general categories under which particular entities fall. A cricket ball is a thing, an object. In contrast, the cricket ball's spherical shape and red colour are not objects but properties of an object. Here you have two ontological categories: objects and properties. Are there others?

This Element addresses ways philosophers have thought about the ontology of relations. Do relations make up a distinctive category of being or are they assimilated into other categories? Are relations a species of property, for instance? Granted, we speak freely of relations, but are relations really out there? Are relations somethings? Are relations entities in their own right? Disagreements are inevitable, but maybe not irresolvable.

Tackling these questions requires some familiarity with ways relations are commonly classified and distinguished from one another and from non-relations. The taxonomy provided in Sections 2 and 3 is meant to be metaphysically neutral and, as far as possible, uncontroversial. The subsequent discussion, indeed the Element as a whole, does not aim at being either impartial or exhaustive. The aim is to give you a visceral sense of the terrain and put you in a position to develop an informed opinion on the matter.

You come to understand the nature of something by starting with examples that point you in the right direction but that ultimately prove unrevealing, even misleading. The process continues until, with perseverance and a measure of luck, you find your way to something closer to the truth. This approach is borrowed from The Philosopher.

> When the objects of an inquiry, in any department, have principles, conditions, or elements, it is through acquaintance with these that knowledge . . . is attained. . . . The natural way of doing this is to start with the things that are more knowable and obvious to us and proceed toward those that are more knowable and clearer by nature; for the same things are not 'knowable relative to us' and 'knowable' without qualification. In the present inquiry we must follow this method and advance from what is more obscure by nature, but clearer to us, towards what is more clear and more knowable by nature. (Aristotle, *Physics* 184a 1–20 in McKeon 1941: 218)

Owing to advances in the sciences, changes in philosophical fashion, and a protean sense of what is obviously the case, this exercise must be begun anew and followed out in every generation. For some it is a waste of time, for others it is a not unpleasant diversion, and for a few it is of the utmost importance. You will begin to appreciate where you lie on this spectrum if you are patient and stay with me to the end. Look at it this way: if you learn nothing else along the way, you stand to learn something about yourself.

So much for preliminaries. Now, take a deep breath, gird yourself, and dive in.

2 Properties and Relations

You can get a feel for what philosophers are talking about when they hold forth on relations, by considering the everyday distinction between properties and relations. A property belongs to an object, a relation stands between objects. A cricket ball's red colour and its spherical shape are properties of the cricket ball. The ball's being on a shelf and its being next to a shoe are relations between the ball and the shelf, in the first instance, and, in the second instance, between the ball and a shoe.

To describe the scene adequately, you would need to mention not simply the ball, the shelf, and the shoe but to say, in addition, how they are related. The shelf, the ball, and the shoe could be on the scene without the ball's being on the shelf or next to a shoe. The point is perfectly general. To describe the cosmos, it would not be enough to list all the things the cosmos contains. You would need to say how these are related. Talk of relations is evidently unavoidable.

2.1 Adicity

Relations differ from properties, then, in holding, not *of*, but *between* or *among* whatever they relate, their *relata*. Relations differ among themselves as well. These differences fall along diverse dimensions. One of these is the 'place' or 'adicity' dimension. The relation of *being on* that holds between the ball and the shelf, and the relation of *being next to* that holds between the ball and a shoe are both two-place relations holding between two relata. The ball's being between one shoe and another shoe is a three-place relation.

Although we rarely speak of four-, or five-, or more place relations, there is no reason to think that relations could not be of any adicity. Our lacking names for such relations reflects, not on reality, but on constraints imposed by finite minds. Rather than learn endless words standing for endless complex relations, we deploy *descriptions* of complex relations. You could invent a word expressing the relation born by the constituents of an organic molecule – and in fact scientists might have reason to do so – but in most cases it is more efficient and less confusing simply to spell out all the ways in which the constituents are related.

At the outset I distinguished properties from relations by observing that a property belongs to an object, while a relation holds between, or among objects. Properties are *monadic*, relations are *polyadic*. You might question this assertion. Lewis Carroll stands in the relation of identity to Charles Dodgson: Carroll *is* Dodgson. Identity is a relation that holds exclusively between something and itself. So, is identity a *monadic*, one-place relation? Or is its appearing to be a relation an artefact of language stemming from the fact that we need some way of indicating when distinct names have the same referents?

Whether you think of identity as a monadic relation or think of identity in some other way would seem to be largely terminological. If identity is a relation, it might be a kind of limiting case, just as the empty set is a limiting case in set theory.

I should warn you, however, that some philosophers will disagree, arguing that there are many monadic relations. The idea of a monadic relation, they insist, is not a big deal. Philosophical differences of this kind reflect fundamental disagreements over the nature of properties and relations. These will be addressed in due course (beginning with Section 4).

Another point over which philosophers disagree in discussions of the adicity of relations is whether some relations are 'multi-grade', whether one and the same relation could have more than one adicity. Think of the *next to* relation. One thing can be next to one thing, or two things, or many things. Does this mean that the next to relation is multi-grade?

Once the question arises, you can see candidate multi-grade relations everywhere. Being one metre apart can hold between two or many objects. Two stones might be a metre apart, but imagine a stone surrounded by a circle of stones each one metre from the central stone. The stone bears the relation to many stones. Similarly, an effect might require one or many causes. Does this mean that distance and causal relations are multi-grade?

David Armstrong is one philosopher who denies that relations could be multi-grade (Armstrong 1997: 85). Armstrong's relations are universals, a topic that will be covered in Section 4, but his central idea, what he calls the Principle of Instantial Invariance, is that if R_1 and R_2 are literally *the same* relation, they, R_1 and R_2, could not have different adicities. Consider the *next to* relation that holds between the cricket ball and a certain shoe. This is a dyadic, two-place relation. Now consider the ball's being next to a shoe and, in addition, being next to another ball. Is this an instance of the same relation having two relata in the first case and three in the second? Or is it a case of the ball's standing in the next to relation to the shoe and standing in the same relation to a second ball? That would be Armstrong's view, but others disagree (see, for instance, McBride 2005).

2.2 Relational Properties

Another point of disagreement concerns relational properties. The cricket ball is next to a shoe, so the ball stands in the *next to* relation to the shoe. Does the ball have the *property* of standing next to the shoe? Does the ball, perhaps by virtue of standing in a particular relation, have, in addition, a relational property?

What exactly would such a relational property be? It belongs to the ball, which means that it is monadic. But the ball's having the property requires that it stands in the *next to* relation to the shoe. The property can come and go without the ball's undergoing any intrinsic change. Move the shoe and the ball ceases to have the property of being next to the shoe. Return the shoe to its original position, and the property returns along with the relation.

Ascriptions of relational properties might best be understood as a way of singling out relations in which the focus, for whatever reason, is on one of the parties to the relation, one of the relata. Is there anything more to the ball's having the relational property of being next to the shoe, other than its being next to the shoe?

All this is threatening to take us prematurely into the metaphysical jungle. Before venturing there, I propose to return to the classificatory discussion begun earlier with the aim of mapping the conceptual lay of the land.

2.3 Symmetrical, Non-Symmetrical, Asymmetrical Relations

I have endeavoured to give you a sense of the distinction between properties and relations by noting that objects are bearers of properties, while relations hold between or among objects. You could think of properties as *ways*: ways objects are. If a billiard ball is spherical and red, the ball is the spherical way and the red way: the ball has the property of being red and the property of being spherical.

As the discussion of relational properties makes clear, this is at best a provisional characterisation. If identity is a relation, then it is a relation between something and itself. If objects can have relational properties, these would differ from familiar intrinsic properties – a billiard ball's redness and sphericality, for instance. If the ball's being next to a shoe is a relational property, it is not obviously a way the *ball* is.

Setting these concerns aside temporarily and turning to comparatively less fraught matters, consider the distinction between relations that, as it were, go 'both ways', those that need not, and those that could not. If the ball is next to the shoe, then the shoe is next to the ball. The *next to* relation is *symmetrical*. If a bears the relation to b, then b bears the relation to a. Examples come easily to mind. If Gus is Lilian's sibling, then Lilian is Gus's sibling. If a is similar to b, or similar to b in some respect, b is similar to a in that respect.

I shall have more to say about 'respects' in Section 6.2. First, however, consider relations that are *not* symmetrical. Suppose Rebecca admires Boris. It need not be the case that Boris admires Rebecca. Boris might or might not return Rebecca's admiration. The *admires* relation that Rebecca bears to Boris is *non-symmetrical*. Non-symmetrical relations have a 'direction'. If Rebecca admires Boris, the relation of admiration runs from Rebecca to Boris. Unlike the next to relation, if a admires b, b might or might not admire a. If Rebecca greets Boris, Boris might or might not reciprocate. If a leans against b, b might or might not lean against a. A playing card might lean against a glass without the glass returning the favour, but two playing cards could lean against one another so as to remain upright.

Asymmetrical relations are a species of non-symmetrical relation. An asymmetrical relation goes in only one direction. If Ben Nevis is taller than Sgùrr Alasdair, Sgùrr Alasdair cannot be taller than Ben Nevis. Bioengineering and time travel aside, if Susan is the mother of Rebecca, Rebecca cannot be the mother of Susan. If today's lunch occurs after breakfast, breakfast cannot occur after lunch.

Non-symmetrical relations of both kinds have *converses*. If Rebecca admires Boris, Boris is admired by Rebecca. Often relations and their converses have distinct labels. If the lintel is *above* the door, the door is *beneath* the lintel. If Rebecca is Susan's daughter, Susan is Rebecca's mother. You could make this explicit: Susan stands in the is-the-mother-of relation to Rebecca, and Rebecca stands in the is-the-daughter-of relation to Susan.

You could think of converses, not as distinct relations, but as a single relation regarded from the perspective of one or the other relata. Complications arise when relata themselves are asymmetrical. You can be *behind* me with or without my thereby being *in front* of you. If my back is turned to you and you are facing me, you are behind me and I am in front of you. If we are facing away from one another, each of us is behind the other. If you are walking *ahead* of me, I am walking *behind* you. But if we are walking in opposite directions, each of us could be walking behind the other.

So is Susan's being the mother of Rebecca the same relation as Rebecca's being the daughter of Susan? Some philosophers have doubted it. *Is the mother of* and *is the daughter of* are clearly different. Susan is the mother of Tim, but Tim is not the daughter of Susan. Might *being the mother of Rebecca* be a property uniquely possessed by Susan? Again, it would seem that there is nothing more to Susan's possessing the property of being the mother of Rebecca than Susan's standing in the *mother of* relation to Rebecca.

Many relations that are non-symmetrical but not asymmetrical have an interesting feature. Rebecca can admire Boris, and Boris can admire Rebecca, but Boris can also admire himself. In this case, like that of the identity relation, something bears the relation to itself. The difference is that the identity relation, if in fact it is a relation, can hold *only* between something and itself. In addition to admiring himself, Boris can admire others, but Boris, like everything else, is identical with himself and nothing else: only Boris is Boris.

Would this make *admires* a multi-grade relation? The relation can hold between two persons, for instance, between persons and themselves, or between a person and many other persons (and vice versa). So, is the relation multi-grade: one-place, two-place, many-place? Like Armstrong, you might resist this thought. Boris's admiring himself could be thought to be a different relation to Rebecca's admiring Boris. Alternatively, you might regard admires as a two-place relation, but one in which the relata can be a single individual, as when Boris admires himself. If Boris admires many people, he stands in the same two-place relation with many people.

A better way to think about such matters would be to start with an assessment of what makes it the case that *a* admires *b* (when *b* might or might not be *a*): *a*'s admiring *b* is a matter of *a*'s harbouring a species of favourable attitude towards *b*, and *b*'s being the object of this attitude. The object of the attitude could be almost anything, existing or not, including the agent to whom it belongs. Thus, *a* could admire Dorothea, a fictional character. What makes it the case that *a* and *b* stand in this relation is just *a*'s having an attitude of admiration towards *b*. Their standing in the relation is not obviously anything more than *a*'s having the attitude.

Can every non-symmetrical relation that is not asymmetrical hold between something and itself? Probably not. Boris could be both the hugger and the one hugged; Boris could smite himself as well as smite others; Boris can see others and, in looking into a mirror, he can see himself. Two playing cards could lean against one another, thereby remaining upright, but a playing card cannot remain upright by leaning against itself.

3 Internal and External Relations

To the extent that they reflect ways relations are commonly classified, the distinctions introduced in Section 2 are relatively uncontroversial. Matters are different when it comes to *internal* and *external* relations. An internal relation is one in which, if you have the relata, you thereby have the relation. Some philosophers characterise internal relations as *necessitated* (David Armstrong) by, or *supervenient* on (David Lewis), their relata (see, for instance, Armstrong 1989: ch. 6; 2004: § 4.6; and Lewis 1986b: 62). What necessitation amounts to will emerge gradually. I shall have more to say about supervenience in Section 5.2.

The similarity relation would qualify as internal in this sense. If you have two red billiard balls, you have each one being similar to the other. The balls are similarly coloured, similarly shaped, and they have similar weights. If identity is a relation between something and itself, then, if you have a something, any something at all, that something is identical with itself.

Notice, incidentally, that *a*'s being identical *to b*, differs from *a*'s being identical *with b*. If *a* and *b* are exactly similar *a* is identical *to b*. Mike is identical *to*, not *with*, his twin, Ike. 'Identical to' expresses the similarity relation. 'Identical with' expresses selfsameness, what philosophers call strict identity.

Sadly, many English speakers, including philosophers writing on the topic, are apparently oblivious to this useful grammatical distinction. You will find philosophers proclaiming that the Morning Star is identical to the Evening Star, when they mean that the Morning Star is identical with the Evening Star: the Morning Star and the Evening Star are two names for a single celestial body, the planet Venus.

Internal relations, including similarity relations, would appear to be founded in their relata in the sense that they are 'no additions of being'. This is how Armstrong and Lewis see it. All you need in order to bring an internal relation on the scene are the relata. External relations, in contrast, might be thought of as something *in addition to* whatever they relate.

Spatial relations are most often mentioned as examples of external relations. Suppose two billiard balls are one metre apart. You could have the billiard balls, just as they are intrinsically, without their being so related. During a game of billiards, spatial relations among billiard balls, but not the balls themselves, are in flux. For it to be the case that two billiard balls are a metre apart, you need more than the balls; you need to locate them a metre apart.

Some philosophers hold that, despite appearances, all relations are internal. This doctrine is often associated with F. H. Bradley, who is depicted as concluding from this that relations are unreal, belonging only to appearances, not to reality (Bradley 1893).

This leaves us with three questions:

(i)   What are internal relations, and how do they differ from external relations?
(ii) Are all relations internal?
(iii) If all relations are internal, does it follow that relations are unreal – would this eliminate relations?

Lurking in the background is the sixty-four dollar ontological question: if relations are not mere appearances, *what* are they? Are relations substances, property-bearing entities? Are they properties borne by substances? Are relations neither substances nor properties, but a distinct category of being?

3.1 Moore and Russell on Internal and External Relations

One way to approach these questions begins with G. E. Moore's important and influential discussion of internal and external relations (Moore 1919). In the course of his discussion, Moore teases out an ambiguity in the way I earlier characterised internal relations: an internal relation is one in which, if you have the relata, you thereby have the relation.

Moore's (1919) Aristotelian Society paper, 'External and Internal Relations', is a broadside against the doctrine – or, as he reckons, the dogma – that all relations are internal. His principal target is Bradley, who, according to Moore, holds that all relations are 'intrinsical'. With his characteristic zeal and his flair for exhaustive (and exhausting) discussions of philosophical topics, Moore explicates internal relations by way of a discussion of relational *properties*. Suppose *a* bears relation *R* to *b* (Susan is the mother of Rebecca), then, Moore would say, *a* has the relational property of bearing *R* to *b* (Susan has the relational property of being the mother of Rebecca).

Moore begins by setting out two principles:

(i) If *a*'s bearing *R* to *b* is an internal relation, then, if anything, *x*, fails to have the relational property of bearing *R* to *b*, then *x* is not *a*: $x \neq a$. (If Susan's being the mother of Rebecca is an internal relation, then, if anything, *x*, fails to have the property of being the mother of Rebecca, then *x* is not Susan.)

(ii) If *a* has the property of bearing *R* to *b*, then anything, *x*, lacking this property *could not* be *a*. (If Susan has the property of being the mother of Rebecca, then she could not have failed to have this property.)

Moore characterises the doctrine that all relations are internal as one according to which (i), which he regards as benign, is taken to entail (ii), which he regards as patently false (or at least at odds with common sense).

Puzzled? What does *a*'s having or lacking a relational property have to do with *a*'s standing in an internal relation to *b*? Seeing what Moore is getting at can help illuminate the territory (but it will not be a stroll in the park).

Start with the thought expressed in (i) that, if *a* has a property, φ, that *b* lacks, then, trivially, *a* is not *b* ($a \neq b$). This, however, does not entail (ii), that is, it does not entail that, had something, *x*, lacked φ, *x* would not have been *a*. Moore's idea is that (ii) amounts to the claim that *a* could not have existed without being φ. Any property, φ, that satisfied (ii) would be 'internal' to its bearer, or, as some would put it, φ is essential to *a*. Moore understands the claim that all relations are internal to amount to the claim that every relational property is internal to its bearer in the sense that its bearer could not have failed to have the property.

Moore's idea can be illustrated by considering a simple case involving ordinary monadic properties. If this ball is red, it follows that anything that is not red is not this ball. This is an instance of (i). What does not follow from (i), however, is that any ball that failed to be red could not have been this ball, that is, the ball could not have existed without being red, an instance of (ii). That would be false because you could have painted the ball white, for instance. The ball's colour is a property of the ball, but a contingent property, a property the ball could have lacked. Were you to paint the ball, the ball, but not the ball's colour, would survive.

You can see how this would apply straightforwardly to relations. If a relation is internal, Moore argues, you could not have had *these* relata without having this relation. Recall my initial characterisation of an internal relation as one in which, if you have the relata, you thereby have the relation. Moore's focus is on the relata: Rebecca and Susan, the two balls. Although it might be terrible to contemplate, Susan could have existed without having given birth to Rebecca, without having the relational property of being Rebecca's mother. On such a conception of internal relations, is the mother of, and is the same colour as, would not count as internal relations.

Moore observes that there is another way of spelling out what it means to say that an internal relation is one in which, if you have the relata, you have the relation. Bertrand Russell, for instance, characterises internal relations by appealing to the 'natures' of the relata. An internal relation, Russell says, is 'grounded in the natures of the related terms' (Russell 1910: 160 [1966: 139]). Moore understands Russell's natures to amount to an object's complement of intrinsic qualities, that is, its complement of *non-relational* properties. Being red and being spherical are intrinsic properties of a billiard ball. Being next to another billiard ball would not be an intrinsic property of the ball.

An internal relation, on Russell's view, is one 'grounded in' properties, not the properties' bearers. If you have two red balls, the balls bear various similarity relations to one another owing to their properties. The balls could have failed to be red, perhaps, but given that they are red, they are similar by virtue of their respective colours being similar. The idea that an internal relation is one in which, if you have the relata, you have the relation, is understood as, if you have these very relata, *just as they are non-relationally*, you have the relation.

On Moore's account the taller than relation would be an external relation. Barack is taller than Boris, but Barack and Boris could have had different heights. You could have Barack and Boris without Barack's being taller than Boris. For Russell, the taller than relation would count as internal. You could have had Barack and Boris without the one's being taller than the other, but you could not have had Barack and Boris *with their respective heights* without Barack's being taller than Boris.

As Moore sees it, whether you characterise internal relations as he does or as Russell does, it is obvious that not all relations are internal; some relations are external. Intrinsically indiscernible objects can stand in different spatial relations, for instance. A complete accounting of the intrinsic, non-relational characteristics of objects would reveal nothing about their spatial relations.

Suppose Barack and Boris are seated two metres apart. Barack has the relational property of being two metres from Boris. You could have Barack and Boris, just as they are intrinsically, however, without their being two metres apart. Moore's way of characterising internal relations yields many more external relations than Russell's, but, on either conception, not all relations are internal: some relations are external.

4 Metaphysical Preliminaries

Moore's discussion of relations is replete with references to relational properties, a species of property discussed briefly in Section 2.2. What is a relational property? In posing this question, I am not asking for examples – Susan's having the property of being the mother of Rebecca, Barack's having the property of being taller than Boris. I am asking for an account of *what it is* for Susan and Barack to have these properties, an account of the *ontology* of relational properties.

One way to approach the ontological question is to ask, given that it is true that Susan has the property of being the mother of Rebecca, or simply the property of being a mother, what *makes* it true, what are the *truthmakers* for this and other true ascriptions of relational properties? Answering this question requires a brief foray into the ontology of properties, relational and otherwise.

Consider a particular ripe tomato. The tomato is red and roughly spherical. The tomato's redness and its sphericality are properties of the tomato. The tomato *has* these properties along with many others. Properties belong to (or 'inhere in') objects, what philosophers call *substances*. Properties are ways substances are. On such a conception, substance and property are what C. B. Martin calls 'correlatives' (Martin 1980, 2008). Every property belongs to some substance, and every substance is propertied. Every property is a way some substance is, and every substance is some way or ways.

Some, maybe most, philosophers today take properties to be *universals*, a special category of general entity capable of being wholly present in distinct places (and times). The tomato *shares* the property of being red with many things – other tomatoes, cricket balls, pillar boxes, traffic lights. All these things have *the same* property: one property, many individual instances, many cases of red. If properties are universals each of these cases is literally one and the same entity (see, for instance, Armstrong 1989).

Although, in some circles, 'property' is synonymous with 'universal', other philosophers accept Locke's dictum: 'All things that exist are only particulars' (Locke 1690: III, iii, 6). This is the view that there are no general *entities*, only general *terms*. The idea that properties are a species of general entity is a product of a perennial tendency to move directly from linguistic categories to categories of being, a topic to which I shall return in Section 4.2. First, however, I propose to look more closely at properties regarded, not as general entities, but as fully particular.

Properties so construed are what Aristotle called *individual accidents* and later philosophers called *modes*. A mode is a modification of something, a substance. A mode depends for its existence on the substance it modifies. A mode has the character of a dent in an automobile fender (the example comes from Cook 1968: 8, 10–11). The tomato's redness and sphericality are particular modifications of the tomato. Objects 'share' properties or have 'the same' property only in the sense that they have *similar* properties. Five red tomatoes have the same colour in the way members of a sports team have the same uniforms.

Philosophers who regard properties as universals or as modes (or accidents, I shall use 'mode' and 'accident' interchangeably) accept a substance–property ontology. Properties require substances, and every substance is propertied. Not all philosophers agree. Some philosophers have thought that objects are nothing in addition to their properties: objects are 'bundles' of properties (Hume 1788; Williams 1953). To say that a property belongs to an object, is just to say that it is a part of the object. There is no more to an object or a substance than its properties. An influential latter-day advocate of this view, D. C. Williams, called properties so regarded, tropes, to distinguish them from properties understood as universals or modes (Williams 1953).

Most philosophers who fly under the banner of trope theory are bundle theorists. Most, but not all. Armstrong (1989: 136) argues that 'we do better, with Locke and C. B. Martin, to hold the trope view in a substance–attribute form'. On Martin's view, tropes belong to substances, they are 'something about' a substance or, as I put it earlier, a particular way a substance is (see Martin 1980, 2008; Heil 2003: 137–50). Because Martin's tropes are in fact modes, I shall use 'trope' to mean what Williams means.

The idea that objects are nothing more than bundles of properties does not sit well with a conception of properties as universals. If an object were nothing more than a bundle of universals, two objects sharing the same properties would in fact be a single object. To be multiply located, universals require anchors, and these could not themselves be universals. If you regard properties as universals, then, you need things that are not universals to account for the multiplicity of objects that populate the cosmos. For a friend of universals, this is the job of substances. Substances function as *particularisers*.

I should warn you that my discussion is far from exhaustive. I am ignoring various competing accounts of universals, for instance. (Armstrong 1989 provides an accessible survey; Keinänen and Tahko 2019; Maurin in press; and Perovic in press discuss the prospects for a one-category ontology of universals.) The point, however, is simply to set out two approaches to properties – as universals and as particulars – so as to keep the discussion from becoming hopelessly abstract.

4.1 Relational Properties Again

Properties, then, have been regarded as universals and as particulars (accidents, modes, or tropes). If properties are universals or modes (or accidents), they belong to substances. If properties are tropes, they combine to make up objects. This yields a three-fold taxonomy of properties as depicted in Figure 1.

Where do relational properties belong? Return to Susan's having the property of being a mother. Susan's possessing this property evidently requires that she stand in the mother-of relation to someone. Suppose she stands in this relation to Rebecca. Then, in addition to Susan's having the relational property of being the mother of Rebecca, Rebecca has the complementary relational property of being the daughter of Susan. The properties belong to Susan and Rebecca respectively. Are these relational properties modes, tropes, or universals? Or are they something else?

No single answer recommends itself. Perhaps this is because relational properties can be accommodated by any of the conceptions of properties on offer: a feature, not a bug. What is unsettling about relational properties is their very innocuousness. What more is there to having a relational property than standing in a particular relation? By virtue of standing in the mother-of relation to Rebecca, Susan has the property of being the mother of Rebecca, and Rebecca, the property of being the daughter of Susan.

This has the aroma of philosophical double-talk. As I observed in Section 2.2, from the perspective of serious ontology, attributing relational properties to something might simply be an affected and needlessly indirect way of indicating that something is party to a given relation. To say that Susan has the property of being a mother, is just to reflect on Susan's standing in the mother–of relation. Why then would anyone want to embrace relational

Properties

	General	Particular
Substance	universals	modes, accidents
Bundle	×	tropes

Figure 1 A taxonomy of properties

properties? The time has come to introduce you to one of the quirks of contemporary metaphysics.

4.2 Linguisticised Metaphysics

Before getting down to business, a word is in order concerning my tendentious use of the label 'linguisticised metaphysics'. In my more cynical moments, I think of philosophers working in metaphysics today as falling into two camps. On one side, there are those (the 'bad' ones) who would regard the phrase 'linguisticised metaphysics' as a pleonasm on a par with 'round circle'. On the other side, there are philosophers (the 'upstanding' ones) who would regard the phrase as an oxymoron. A harsh (and pointlessly offensive) assessment, no doubt, but it gives you, the reader, advance warning and equips you to decide which of my many opinions to embrace, which to discount, and which to ignore altogether.

In setting out the range of views on properties, I neglected to mention one that has had scores of devoted adherents. The omitted position, 'nominalism', amounts to a kind of null hypothesis about properties: something's possessing a property is a matter of a predicate's holding true of the something and nothing more. Any true attribution, no matter how contrived, denotes a property.

Suppose it is true of a particular tomato in a supermarket bin that it is spherical, that it costs less than a pineapple, that it has been handled by more than four people, and that it is next to a stray avocado. In that case, the tomato has the property of being spherical, the property of costing less than a pineapple, the property of having been handled by four people, the property of being next to an avocado, as well as endless other properties.

We talk this way in everyday life when we are not engaged in metaphysical reflection, and it is harmless enough for everyday purposes. When you take up metaphysics, matters are different. It is bad enough to suppose that whenever a predicate holds true of an object it denotes a property, but nominalists go further and insist that this is all there is to objects' possessing properties. You have objects, and these objects answer to various predicates. The tomato answers to the predicate 'is spherical' and to the predicate 'is red'. But the tomato's redness and sphericality are not distinct features of the tomato answering to 'is red' and 'is spherical'. The predicates apply *holus bolus* to the tomato. If you have a view of this kind, relational properties are there for the asking, but in that case, there are no theres there. Properties are not ways objects are. Properties are shadows cast by predicates.

This case is one in which ontology – in this instance the ontology of properties – is read off forms of speech we deploy in describing and explaining the cosmos. I believe, and I have some confidence that you will agree, that onto-logically serious talk of properties reflects something about the make-up of objects. 'Is red' is true of the tomato, not *holus bolus*, but because of some way the tomato is. 'Is spherical' is true of the tomato because of some *other* way the tomato is. These ways the tomato is would appear to be properties in any of the senses introduced earlier.

What distinguishes cases in which a predicate picks out a genuine property from cases in which a predicate holds true of an object, but not because the predicate designates a property possessed by the object? This is a difficult topic, but I can mention one widely accepted criterion that goes back at least to Plato: genuine properties make a causal difference to their bearers.

A cricket ball's sphericality empowers it to roll, to make a circular concave impression in the turf, to feel spherical when you pick it up. Its redness affects the way it reflects ambient light radiation so as to look red. In contrast, the ball's having been made in Moorabbin, and its costing $12, although true of the ball, make no difference to what the ball does or could do. A duplicate ball, not made in Moorabbin and not costing $12, would comport itself no differently than this one does.

What of the ball's being one metre from your shoe, a candidate relational property? Your shoe and the cricket ball exert minute gravitational forces on one another, forces that vary with distance. These forces, however, have their source in the respective masses of the ball and your shoe, not in the relational property of being a metre apart.

The case appears representative of relational properties generally. You might balk at the causal measure of propertyhood, replacing it with something that allows relational properties to count as genuine properties, but you would be left with an embarrassing discrepancy between relational and non-relational prop-erties. You would be left, as well, with the task of explaining why relational properties are needed at all if their presence or absence makes no difference to what their bearers do or could do.

Is this too quick? Susan's having or lacking the property of being the mother of Rebecca is decidedly significant, especially to Rebecca and Susan. The question, however, is not whether Susan's being the mother of Rebecca is or is not significant, but whether its significance turns on Susan's possession of a relational property.

Ask yourself what more there is to having a relational property than standing in a particular relation. Susan possesses the relational property of being the mother of Rebecca if, and only if, Susan stands in the mother-of relation to Rebecca. Attributing the relational property to Susan (and the complementary property of being the daughter of Susan to Rebecca) would seem to be nothing more than an oblique way of indicating that Susan stands in the mother-of relation to Rebecca.

Talk of relational properties is another case in which philosophers move from ordinary forms of speech, which, after all, serve many purposes, directly to ontology. If I accomplish nothing else in this Element, I hope to convince you (if you were not convinced already) that this kind of linguisticised metaphysics is a bad idea. The question to ask, is not whether a particular predicate – 'is the mother of', for instance – applies truly to an object, but, when it applies truly, what its truthmaker is, what must be the case if Susan is Rebecca's mother. The truthmaker for 'Susan has the property of being Rebecca's mother ' is simply Susan's standing in the mother-of relation to Rebecca.

5 Truthmaking

Although I have appealed to truthmakers and truthmaking in characterising relations, I have postponed an explicit discussion of truthmaking, and in particular the truthmaking relation. One reason for deferring the discussion is that truthmaking is one of those notions the simplicity of which makes it more difficult to characterise than to deploy. By now, however, you are familiar enough with the deployment and ready for an account of what is being deployed.

Start with the thought that, when a judgement is true, something makes it true. If the assertion that snow is white is true, it is made true by snow's being white. If it is true that Susan is Rebecca's mother, this is made true by Susan's being the mother of Rebecca. If it is true that Boris's brain was hijacked by aliens from another galaxy, this would be true by virtue of Boris's brain's having been hijacked by aliens from another galaxy.

In each of these cases you have a truth and something that makes it the case that the truth is true. Truths that are up for consideration are embodied by *truth bearers*. Truths can be expressed by written sentences and utterances of sentences, but truth bearers cannot be straightforwardly identified with either of these. A candidate truth bearer must be 'truth evaluable', capable of being true or false. To be truth evaluable, a truth bearer must be something meaningful, and neither inscriptions nor utterances are in themselves meaningful. Their meaning is inherited from . . .

From what?

This is not the place to delve into theories of meaning, so I propose to use the word 'judgement' as a stand-in for *whatever it is* that sentences and utterances express and equips them to be true or false. You might express your judgement that snow is white by uttering or writing out the sentence 'Snow is white'.

Others might express the same judgement by uttering the sentence '*La neige est blanche*' or the sentence '*Schnee ist weiß*'.

This gives us at least a name for one side, the truth-bearer side, of the truthmaking relation. What of the other side, the side that makes a judgement true? David Armstrong argues that truthmakers are 'states of affairs' in his proprietary sense, snow's being white, for instance (see Armstrong 1997, 2004). For Armstrong, a state of affairs is a substance's having a property – Armstrong's properties being universals – at a particular time. On this view, states of affairs are the building blocks of the cosmos. An ordinary object comprises distinct states of affairs that share a single substance.

Whatever there is to be said for this proposal, it would be a bad idea to yoke the truthmaking to any particular ontology. Philosophers can agree on the significance of truthmaking without agreeing on the ontology of truthmakers. Leaving the ontological details to one side, truthmakers, at least for truths pertaining to the cosmos, are ways the cosmos is. Snow's being white is one way the cosmos is, and this way is an apt truthmaker for the judgement that snow is white. Notice that this leaves open what snow's being white *is*, the nature of snow and its properties. That, presumably, is something you would need to turn to chemistry, and ultimately to physics, to discover.

Truthmaking, then, is a relation between a truth bearer and some way the cosmos is. At least this is so for truths concerning the cosmos. Might there be truths, useful and important truths, uncontroversial truths that lack truthmakers? Consider truths of mathematics. What makes it true that $7 + 5 = 12$? What makes the Pythagorean theorem true? Ross Cameron and Agustín Rayo contend that, although such truths apply in the cosmos, they do so 'trivially': they ask nothing of the cosmos, they do not require the cosmos to be any one way rather than another (Cameron 2010; Rayo 2010).

You can see their point by asking yourself whether the cosmos could have turned out in such a way that $7 + 5 \neq 12$. Imagine God setting out to create the cosmos ex nihilo. God could choose not to give electrons unit negative charge, or elect not to make electrons at all, but $7 + 5 = 12$ is true whatever cosmos God decides to create.

This point should not be confused with another, quite different point. God might have been able to create a cosmos in which, whenever seven things are put together with five things, they spawn an additional thing. In such a cosmos, when you put seven eggs in a carton and add five more, an additional egg suddenly appears. This would not make it the case that $7 + 5 \neq 12$ or that $7 + 5 = 13$, however, it would simply be an interesting fact about causal processes operative in the cosmos.

Might truths of mathematics have truthmakers *outside* the cosmos? Might there be an eternal immutable realm of numbers that supplies truthmakers for mathematical truths? If mathematics asks nothing of the cosmos, why should it constrain entities that exist in some fashion apart from the cosmos? It is likely that the idea that every truth requires a truthmaker, truthmaker universalism, is what is calling the shots here: if there are no candidate truthmakers in the cosmos, there must be truthmakers residing outside the cosmos.

John Bigelow accepts a version of truthmaker universalism in the form of what he calls the Truthmaker Axiom (or simply Truthmaker): 'whenever something is true, there must be something in the world which makes it true' (Bigelow 1988: 122). If mathematical truths are true, then there must be something *in* the world that makes them true.

Bigelow then appeals to entailment to explicate truthmaking. David Lewis follows suit (Lewis 2001). Bigelow puts it this way:

> whenever something is true, there must be something whose existence entails that it is true. The 'making' in 'making true' is essentially logical entailment ... . Suppose there to be something which is proposed as a truthmaker for some truth. And suppose it is admitted that the existence of that thing does not entail the truth in question. This means that it is logically possible for that thing still to exist, even if what is actually true had not been true. In the actual world, *a* exists and *A* is true, say; but in some other possible world *a* might still exist, even though *A* is not true. There must surely be some difference between these two possible worlds! So there must be something in one of these worlds which is lacking in the other, and which accounts for this difference in truth. ... If something is true, then there must be, that is to say there must exist, something which makes the actual world different from how it would have been if this had not been true. (Bigelow 1988: 125–6)

So does the truthmaking relation amount to entailment? One reason to doubt that this is so is that entailment is a relation between items having truth values: if p entails q, then p could not be true if q is false; p's being true necessitates q's truth. Truthmaking would seem to be a *cross-categorial* relation, however, a relation between a truth bearer and some way the cosmos is. A way the cosmos is, snow's being white, for instance, is not something that itself could be true or false.

Taking the point, Bigelow adds: 'Truthmaker should not be construed as saying that an *object* entails a truth; rather it requires that the proposition *that that object exists* entails the truth in question' (Bigelow 1988: 126). So talk of objects entailing the truth of judgements is to be understood as an abbreviated way of saying that propositions or judgements that those objects exist entail the truth of the judgements in question.

This refinement of Truthmaker resolves the mystery of how a way the cosmos is could entail a truth, but it introduces a new difficulty. Snow does not entail that snow is white is true; rather, the judgement, or, as Bigelow would have it, the proposition that snow, which is white, exists, entails that the judgement is true. In order to perform this service, however, the proposition must be true, made true, presumably, by snow or by snow's being white. This simply reinstates the original question, what is the truthmaking relation? Invoking entailment is suggestive, perhaps, but ultimately unhelpful.

A related worry attends efforts to locate truthmakers for negative existential judgements, for instance, 'there are no arctic penguins'. The judgement is true, but what makes it true, what is its truthmaker? Does the cosmos contain, in addition to penguins, non-existent arctic penguins or arctic penguin absences?

One attempt to resolve the problem posits a 'totality' or 'that's all' fact. A list of things in your top dresser drawer does not suffice for the truth of 'there are no cats in the drawer'. For that, you would need more than the absence of cats on the list, you would need to add that the list is complete: 'the drawer contains socks, handkerchiefs, and gloves *and that is all*'. 'That is all' is not made true solely by what is the case, but by an additional totality fact. You have the fact that this is what there is *and* the fact that this is all there is.

True, an exhaustive inventory of what there is does not entail that this is all there is – hence, that anything not on the inventory does not exist – but this is an artefact of language: linguisticised metaphysics! A *description* of what is the case would not license judgements as to what is not the case without being supplemented by a 'that is all clause'. From this, it does not follow that the cosmos as it in fact is requires an additional totality fact to make it true that this is all there is. In moving from truths about descriptions of the cosmos to the cosmos itself, it is easy to mistake features of descriptions of what is and what is not the case for features of the cosmos (see Heil 2006 for a further discussion).

5.1 The Truthmaking Relation

Suppose, then, that truthmaking is a relation between truths – truth bearers – and ways the cosmos is. What is the nature of the relation? I follow Armstrong in regarding truthmaking as an internal relation between a truth bearer and the cosmos's being as it is (Armstrong 2004: 9, Heil 2000, 2006). If you have a judgement that snow is white and snow is in fact white, then you have snow's being white making the judgement true. I prefer to speak of judgements, rather than propositions. Propositions are philosophical posits, entities with built-in meanings, and it is easy to doubt that there are any such entities. They have all the markings of philosophical sky hooks, items introduced to solve problems that we wish would go away – or are of our own making.

In contrast to the proposition that snow is white, the sentence 'snow is white' – thought, uttered, or written – means what it does owing to its deployment by speakers of English. In invoking judgements I mean to be pointing to meaningful units, however packaged. These are meaningful only because they have a role in the lives of intelligent agents interacting with one another and with their surroundings. When true, judgements constitute truth bearers. Truth bearers and truthmakers are internally related: given the relata you have the relation. If you have a judgement that snow is white and you have snow's being white, you thereby have the judgement's being true.

Is that *it*? Is this what all this toing and froing about truthmaking boils down to? At the outset I noted that simple things are sometimes easier done than said. That is certainly the case with truthmaking. Why then bother? Why subject you to a lengthy discussion if the discussion adds nothing to what you probably knew already? The goal has been to emphasise the importance of the notion of truthmaking and its implications for ontology, including the ontology of relations, and to do so in a way that captures the unmysterious nature of truthmaking.

In Section 5 I observed that it is one thing to know that snow's being white is the truthmaker for the judgement that snow is white, but another matter altogether to know the nature of the truthmaker. For that you need the sciences, ultimately physics. Even in physics, talk of particles might be made true, not by mobile bits of matter, but by disturbances in fields, wrinkles in spacetime, or something wholly surprising. Our ways of thinking and talking take us *to* the cosmos, but do not thereby reveal the nature of the cosmos. This, really, is just another way to say what many philosophers – including Ludwig Wittgenstein, Donald Davidson, and F. H. Bradley – have said in different ways: you cannot read off the nature of things from forms of thought or our ways of talking about those things.

This is something each generation of philosophers must rediscover for itself and recast in a congenial contemporary idiom. The truthmaker for 'snow is white' could turn out to be congeries of colourless particles. In the case of relations, the idea would be that truthmakers for relational truths could turn out to be non-relational features of the cosmos. Were that so, it would not follow that talk of relations is false or meaningless; however, it would illuminate the nature of what makes relational truths true.

Philosophy, and in particular metaphysics, can benefit from judicious applications of a truthmaker principle: if you advance a metaphysical thesis, you owe the rest of us some account of what its truthmaker might be, or, failing that, why it does not require a truthmaker.

5.2 Supervenience: A Brief History

In initiating the discussion of truthmaking earlier, I mentioned John Bigelow's Truthmaker Axiom: 'whenever something is true, there must be something in the world which makes it true'. Truth, Bigelow says, *supervenes* on being, and he glosses supervenience as follows: 'One sort of thing is said to be supervenient on another when you could not have any difference in things of the first sort unless there were some difference in things of the second sort' (Bigelow 1988: 132; see also Lewis 2001).

The *A*s supervene on the *B*s when there could be no *A*-difference without a *B*-difference.

Appeals to supervenience came into prominence in the mid-twentieth century with the moral philosopher, R. M. Hare (1952). Hare argued that moral discourse, our use of moral terms – good, bad, right, wrong – was governed by a supervenience principle: no moral difference without a non-moral, purely natural difference.

Hare's focus was on moral judgements, not states or properties targeted by those judgements. Hare was an anti-realist about moral properties. His contention was that, if you are moved to judge that one person is good and another not good, the two must differ in some non-moral respect. What makes a judgement a moral judgement is its expressing a moral attitude that is sensitive to non-moral factual differences. This is a defeasible substantive thesis about constraints on moral judgements that was subsequently extended to cover normative judgements generally.

Supervenience was appropriated by Donald Davidson, who applied it to the relation between the mental and the physical (Davidson 1970). Hare distinguished moral from non-moral, natural discourse. Davidson followed suit in distinguishing mental and physical discourse. Both Hare and Davidson recognised that an analytic reduction of moral or mental predicates to non-moral, physical predicates was not on the cards. For Hare, supervenience amounted to the view that moral judgements, expressions of moral attitudes, were constrained by non-moral facts, a constraint reflected in everyday moral discourse. Davidson embellished this idea. Mental and physical predicates addressed the same subject matter, but in different ways. If it is true that you are in a particular mental state, that very state could be given a non-equivalent physical description.

Hare saw supervenience as capturing an important feature of our moral practices. Davidson's appeal to supervenience stemmed from his conviction that reasons are causes, a controversial thesis at the time. When an agent acts for a reason, the reason must be a cause of the action. Davidson recognised that you can have a reason to A and subsequently A, without A-ing for that reason: you might A for some other reason.

Reasons are states of mind, actions include bodily motions. If, seated in a restaurant, you wave your hand because you want attract a waiter's attention, your waving is caused by your desire to attract the waiter's attention and your belief that you can accomplish this by waving, or perhaps by an intention itself caused by the belief–desire pair. One way to account for mental–physical causal interaction would be to accept mental–physical supervenience: mental states are in fact physical states, states answering to a physical description. There are not two states, one physical and one mental. There is one state describable in two conceptually orthogonal ways.

Attempting to discredit the identification of the mental with the physical by showing that descriptions couched in a mental vocabulary could not be analysed or paraphrased using a physical vocabulary would be beside the point. Mental and physical ascriptions, like their moral and natural counterparts, play by different rules.

Supervenience for Davidson, then, amounts to the precept that whatever makes true the ascription of a state of mind, answers as well to a non-mental, physical description. This is not the thesis that when you are in a position to ascribe a particular mental state to me, you must also be in a position to offer a physical description of that state. All that follows is that there would be some way of singling out the state in a non-mental vocabulary, whether or not you are – or anyone else is – in a position to do so.

This is one aspect of Davidson's (1970: 215) insistence that something is mental or physical 'only as described'. The mental–physical distinction is not a metaphysical distinction between distinct families of property, for instance; it is a distinction between two incommensurable ways of describing a portion of the cosmos. The mental–physical distinction is not what the scholastics called a real distinction, it is not a distinction in reality, but a distinction of reasoned reason, what today would be called a conceptual distinction.

I have spent time on Davidson because his way of thinking about supervenience is naturally expressible by invoking truthmaking. To say that the mental supervenes on the physical is to say that truthmakers for particular assertions concerning minds and their contents could be truly described in a physical vocabulary, ultimately in the vocabulary of physics. The important insight here is that you could be adept at making judgements about states of mind yet have no notion of the nature – the physical nature – of the truthmakers for those judgements.

Does truth supervene on being, then? In light of the foregoing, this is little more than a circuitous way of asserting that truths concerning the cosmos are made true by ways the cosmos is. Substituting supervenience for truthmaking does nothing to illuminate the truthmaking relation. It is, in addition, potentially misleading.

Why misleading? In the 1980s philosophers working in metaphysics and the philosophy of mind called upon supervenience to perform remarkable metaphysical feats. These philosophers spun supervenience into a relation among families of property. They read Davidson's suggestion that the mental supervenes on the physical, not as a conceptual proposal concerning the relation between mental and physical predicates, but as a thesis about a distinctive relation mental properties bear to physical properties.

Davidson's contention that mental predicates could not be analysed or paraphrased in a physical vocabulary was thought to amount to the contention that mental and physical properties were distinct species of property – linguisticised metaphysics strikes again! The assertion that the mental supervened on the physical was repurposed: mental properties are distinct from but in some way dependent on physical properties. The misalignment between mental and physical taxonomies that blocked attempts at reduction bespoke of the 'multiple realisability' of higher-level mental entities. One mental property can have many different lower-level physical 'realisers'. Indeed, owing to non-reducibility, the class of realisers is open-ended. Pain states supervene on physical states (their realisers). But what realises pain in you differs from what realises pain in a lizard, and what realises pain in creatures with a silicone physiology. Pain is thus multiply realisable, as is every other species of mental state.

Reduction, too, took on a metaphysical cast. Reduction as originally deployed by philosophers of science and by Davidson was a matter of analysis or explanation. If the As are reducible to the B's, truths or explanations concerning the As are derivable from, hence replaceable by, B-truths and B-explanations. Here, the A's and B's are laws or predicates. To say that the mental is not reducible to the physical is to say that mental descriptions and explanations cannot be replaced by physical descriptions and explanations – Davidson's point.

In the hands of others, reduction became a relation among entities – properties or states, for instance. If the mental is not reducible to the physical, this means that mental properties or states are not physical properties or states.

5.3 Supervenience as a Metaphysical Relation

All this transforms supervenience into a metaphysical heavyweight. Books and papers were churned out in attempts to explicate the metaphysics of supervenience. Supervenience was quickly seen to extend beyond the mental and the physical to the special sciences, yielding a hierarchy of levels of reality. Entities governed by laws falling under the purview of physics occupy the lowest level. Chemical properties and laws supervene on those in physics, biological properties and laws supervene on chemical properties and laws, and so on, with psychology, sociology, and the social sciences occupying successively higher levels.

On such a view, the job of the various sciences is to discover the properties and laws operative in their respective domains. These depend on, without being reducible to, properties and laws native to lower-level domains. The picture brought with it a momentarily satisfying account of how the various sciences could be autonomous, while still being firmly rooted in physics. Higher-level domains are realised by, but not reducible to, those at lower levels.

The picture also introduced a host of new problems; chief among these being the problem of 'causal relevance'. If higher-level, supervenient properties depend on, while being distinct from, those at lower levels, how could higher-level properties contribute causally to events in which they figured? Any causal contribution they might make would be undercut by the properties on which they supervened, their realisers.

You can see how this works in a simplified case. Suppose your thinking about beetroot sherry leads you to desire a glass of beetroot sherry. Your thought and your desire supervene on lower-level physical states. These states, P^1 and P^2, realise the higher-level mental states (see Figure 2).

Because your thought and desire both supervene on lower-level physical states, your thought could not bring about your desire directly. For your thought to bring about your desire, it would need to bring about your desire's lower-level realiser, P^2 (see Figure 3).

The difficulty now shifts to your thought's causing P^2. Doing so would call for your thought, a higher-level state, to intervene in the causal milieu to which P^2 belongs, which would amount to the usurpation of laws governing lower-

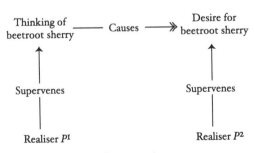

Figure 2 Supervenient states

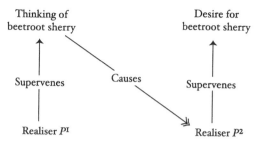

Figure 3 A higher-level state causing another higher-level state by causing its realiser

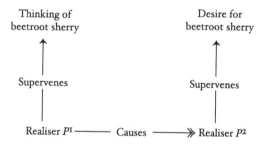

Figure 4 Higher-level states as epiphenomenal

level processes. In fact, what goes for P^2 goes for *its* lower-level realiser and, ultimately, some fundamental physical realiser – a complex arrangement of particles, for instance, or a disturbance in a field.

Your thought's causing your desire, then, would require its intervening in the domain encompassed by physics. Such interventions would play havoc with physics as we know it. We seem to have no choice but to accept the situation depicted in Figure 4.

What began as an effort to accommodate higher-level causal interactions and the laws governing them, thus culminated in making the higher-level domains epiphenomenal, carried along on the backs of domains at lower levels and ultimately on the back of physics.

As Jaegwon Kim, an early influential exponent of supervenience, makes clear, there was little or no consensus as to the nature of the supervenience relation (Kim 1990). In response, some took refuge in the all-purpose philosophical dodge: 'Look, get over it; we *know* that the various sciences track supervenient domains of objects and properties, so it must all work out *somehow*.'

Speaking as someone who devoted far too much time and energy to the futile project of sorting out the metaphysics of supervenience, I am more than happy to throw my lot in with Davidson, leave the topic behind, and stick with unadorned truthmaking. Truthmakers for truths expressible in terms that are at home in the special sciences and in everyday discourse could, in principle, if not in practice, be described in the vocabulary of physics.

6 Bradley's Regress

Discussions of the ontology of relations most often set the table with a consideration of F. H. Bradley's attack on the reality of relations. In Section 3, I observed that Bradley is regularly cast as arguing, first, that all relations are internal, then concluding from this that relations are unreal. Although Bradley does indeed argue for the unreality of relations, as Stewart Candlish makes clear, there is little reason to think that Bradley accepted that all relations are internal and even less reason to think that he would have taken that to imply the unreality of relations (Candlish 2007; Candlish and Basile 2017).

Bradley has suffered the fate of too many philosophers: everyone knows what the position is and what is wrong with it. This saves us from having to wrestle with what Bradley actually says. Candlish puts it this way:

> Despite the efforts of some recent propagandists, most philosophers these days still do not read Bradley. The result is that they are content to work with a stereotype, whose sources and accuracy go unexamined. This stereotype is inaccurate, and most of us have got Bradley wrong. Perhaps this would not matter much if the error had no serious consequences. The problem is, though, that being wrong about Bradley, in the ways in which we *are* wrong about him, does have serious consequences. One is that we misunderstand our own history, and thereby misunderstand ourselves and the nature of what we are about. Another is that we are deprived of one of the opportunities to connect what we do in philosophy with what some of the philosophers of the past have done; we may, in consequence, fall under the impression that only we, and those obviously like us, are really doing philosophy, at least as it ought to be done. (This, a perennial temptation for philosophers, leaves the residual problem of explaining just what these other chaps, who after all were not stupid, were actually doing. But that problem is usually ignored.) But perhaps the most unfortunate consequence is that we may in our ignorance miss some interesting ideas which cannot be found in the modern philosophical canon. (Candlish 1989: 331)

What everyone knows is that Bradley argued that all relations are internal and that this meant that relations could be absorbed into their terms, their relata. Second, Bradley held that accepting the reality of relations portended a regress. Suppose a bears relation R to b and that R is no less a real entity than a and b. In that case, R must be related to a and to b. Call the relations R bears to a and b respectively, R^1 and R^2. But now R^1 and R^2 must be related to R and to both a and b, calling for four additional relations R^3, R^4, R^5, and R^6. This generates a vicious regress, an

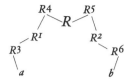

Figure 5 Relations standing in relations to their relata: The first step in Bradley's regress

explosion of relations. The regress is vicious because, before R can relate a and b, R^1 and R^2 must relate R to a and b, and so for R^1, R^2, and R, a, and b (see Figure 5).

6.1 Responses to Bradley: Russell and McTaggart

Hosts of philosophers have responded to this version of the regress. One response, by Russell and echoed by many others, was that the regress was not real, but stemmed from a confusion on Bradley's part. Relations, unlike what they relate, their terms, do not themselves stand in need of being related to their relata. This is what a's bearing R to b amounts to. There is no sense in which in order for a to bear R to b, R must be related to a and b via R^1 and R^2 (and so on).

Russell's response is a non sequitur, however. In attacking the reality of relations, Bradly is taking his opponents at their word. To say that something is real is to say that it is not dependent on anything other than itself. To be real is to be what has traditionally been called a *substance*.

> Russell reminds us that each of his particulars 'stands entirely on its own and is completely self-subsistent', having 'that sort of self-subsistence that used to belong to substance', so that 'each particular that there is in the world does not in any way logically depend upon any other particular' (Russell 1918: 179). (Candlish 2007: 167)

Russell agrees with Bradley that to be real is to be a self-standing entity, and, as Russell himself notes, these are what have traditionally been called substances. So if relations are real, they, or their instances, must be substances, and, as substances, they stand in need of being related to other substances if they are going to function as relations. If a stands in relation R to b, then R, or the instance of R on the scene, if it is real, has the status of a substance, and the regress ensues.

Unlike Russell, J. M. E. McTaggart argued that Bradley's regress was real enough, but benign. Relations generate, but do not depend on infinite chains of relations to do their job.

> If we start with an original relationship, there is the derivative quality of standing in that relationship, the derivative relationship between the substance and that quality, and so on again without end. Moreover, whenever, in

one of these series, we come to a relationship, that relationship generates, besides the quality derivative from it, a relationship derivative from it, and from each of these an infinite series arises, which again divides into two at each member which is a relationship. All the qualities in these infinite series are parts of the nature of the substance possessing them, and that nature therefore is a compound quality with an infinite number of parts.

These infinite series, however, are not vicious, because it is not necessary to complete them in order to determine the meaning of the earlier terms. The meaning of an earlier member in this series does not depend on a later, but, on the contrary, the meaning of any later term depends on that of an earlier term. (McTaggart 1921: § 88; I am grateful to an anonymous referee who pointed me to this passage)

You can get a feel for McTaggart's point by considering the truth regress. Suppose p is true. In that case it is true that p is true, true that it is true that p is true, and so on ad infinitum. The truth of p, however, does not depend on all those other truths; in fact, the reverse is true: they depend on it.

Like Russell, McTaggart fails to appreciate Bradley's position, however. If relations are entities alongside substances and properties, they must stand in relations to whatever they relate. You could have R, a, and b, without a's standing in R to b. To relate a and b, R must stand in an appropriate relation to a and to b, and the regress is up and running. What is crucial here is that, if R is real, if R exists, R's belonging to a special category of relations is beside the point. R's status as a real entity is enough to produce the regress.

6.2 Relations as Tropes

Another response to the regress appeals to tropes. Peter Simons, for instance, has argued that the idea that relations themselves stand in need of relations to their relata stems from the assumption that relations are universals (Simons 2010). Simons's thought is that the regress is a consequence, not of relations being entities, but of their being *general* entities, universals. In that case, you could have a, b, and the relation R, without a's standing in R to b.

This is clear in the case of external relations. Before you could have two billiard balls being a metre apart, you need more than the balls and the metre-apart relation. You need to put the balls into the relation. Were R a universal, you could have a, b, and R without R's relating a and b – if R related c and d, for instance. This creates the impression that a, b, and R need to be put together – *related* – before a bears R to b. You could have Barack, Boris, and the taller-than relation, without Barack's being taller than Boris because many things are taller than other things.

Simons argues that, if R is a trope, a particular entity, and you have R, you thereby have R's relating a and b. R exists only in so far as it relates a and b. R, a trope, is a one-off. R could not have related any other relata. R is 'relata specific': if you have a, b, and R, you thereby have R's relating a and b (Wieland and Betti 2008). The taller-than relation that holds between Barack and Boris is both unique to Barack and Boris and numerically distinct from the taller-than relation that holds between Boris and Rebecca.

Fair enough, but why think that replacing relational universals with relational tropes would block the regress? If relations are tropes, and tropes are real entities, they are on the scene alongside their relata. This would seem to require that they stand in relations to their relata, so the regress would be reinstated. The existence of R's necessitating a's standing in R to b shows, not that R does not itself stand in relations to a and to b, but, at most, that the relations R bears to a and to b are internal relations: if you have a, b, and R, you thereby have a's standing in R to b.

What of internal relations? If a relational trope were internally related to its relata, would that block the regress? You might think so. In the case of an internal relation you need only the items related (just as they are in themselves), to have the relation. Suppose that is so. Suppose that internal relations are nothing in addition to their relata. Take similarity, a paradigmatic internal relation. If a is similar to b, then, if you have the relata, a and b, you have its being true that a and b are similar. Suppose you have two red billiard balls. All you need is the balls, just as they are, for it to be the case that they are similar.

This case illustrates something that surfaced earlier. When ordinary objects are similar, they are most often similar in some respect or respects and not others. A cricket ball and a baseball are similar with respect to their shapes, but not with respect to their colours. The balls' respective shapes are similar without qualification: if you have balls with these shapes, you have the balls' being similar. This is so for complex objects generally. Similarity relations among such objects are indirect, founded on their properties.

Considerations of this kind have encouraged the thought that internal relations are not, after all, real relations. This probably explains why Bradley is so often characterised as holding that all relations are internal, and concluding from this that relations are nothing in addition to their relata. I shall return to Bradley in Section 6.5; first, however, two matters discussed by Fraser MacBride bear mention.

6.3 Truthmaking and Ontological Commitment

MacBride, who has written extensively on relations, makes a point of distinguishing truthmaking from ontological commitment (MacBride 2011, 2020).

Even if it were the case that truthmakers for judgements concerning internal relations are monadic, non-relational features of their relata, relations 'have other theoretical roles, besides truthmaking, to perform' (MacBride 2011: 162).

> A truth-maker for a statement S is (at least) something the existence of which determines (necessitates) that S is true. By contrast, something x is an ontological commitment of S if, roughly speaking, S could not be true unless x existed. Typically, a statement S incurs ontological commitment to an entity or some entities because we refer to it or quantify over them when we make the statement. It's easy to run *truth-making* and *ontological commitment* together but it's important to keep them separate. A statement S cannot be true unless the entities to which S is ontologically committed exist. So it's a *necessary* condition of the truth of S that the entities to which S is ontologically committed exist. By contrast, it's a *sufficient* condition for the truth of S that a truth-maker for S exists because a truth-maker for S determines that S is true. (MacBride 2020: § 3)

Even supposing relations are not required as truthmakers for relational judgements, then, such judgements might nevertheless carry with them ontological commitments to relations.

Consider the judgement that this cricket ball is heavier than that baseball. (As you undoubtedly recall from Section 1, a regulation cricket ball weighs 160 g and a baseball weighs 142 g.) For this judgement to be true, you need only the balls' having their respective weights. The balls' having these weights suffices for the truth of the judgement. This does not mean, however, that the judgement does not commit us to an internal relation between the two *balls*. In making the judgement we commit ourselves to the existence of the two balls, even though the balls are not what makes the judgement true. The balls could have had different weights, so you could have had these balls without the one's being heavier than the other.

This, in effect, resuscitates Moore's argument (Section 3.1). The respective weights of the two balls suffices for the truth of 'the cricket ball is heavier than the baseball'. If you have these weights, you have the one's being heavier than the other. From this, it does not follow that, if you have these balls, you have one's being heavier than the other. These very balls could have had different weights. For it to be true that the one ball is heavier than the other, you need *these* balls having these weights. The heavier-than relation holding between the balls cannot plausibly be dispensed with in favour of the balls, it must be something in addition to the balls.

You might object to this line of reasoning. Yes, the balls could have had different weights, but in judging that one is heavier than the other, you are making a judgement about *these* balls (*with* their respective weights), that the one is heavier than the other. It is true that the heavier-than relation in this case relates the balls only indirectly, only by relating their respective weights, but at least *this* relation is internal: if you have the weights, you have the relation. If a relation is an internal relation, however, it is no less a relation, no less real for that. Relations are back in the picture, and so is Bradley's regress.

6.4 The Ontology of Internal Relations

Are internal relations genuine additions of being, entities, not required as truthmakers for relational judgements, perhaps, but required, even so, for relational judgements to be true? In deploying relational judgements are we ontologically committed to the existence of relations?

Some relations, similarity, for instance, or identity, are apparently recessive. If you have the colours of two red billiard balls you have their being similar. Their similarity requires no further explanation, it rests on no further similarity. There is no more to the two colours' similarity than the colours themselves. The balls inherit their similarity from the similarity of their colours. Similarity judgements are relational in form, but their truth does not appear to rest on an ontological commitment to relational entities.

Matters are different when you move beyond similarity and identity and consider asymmetrical relations such as the heavier-than relation holding between a particular cricket ball and a particular baseball. This relation holds only because the weight of the one is in fact greater than the weight of the other. There is no getting rid of this relation.

If relations are entities, however, what kinds of entity are they? In the *Categories*, Aristotle speaks of 'relatives', by which he means not relations as we denominate them, but relational predications. In saying that a particular cricket ball is heavier than a particular baseball, you are describing the cricket ball *in relation to* the baseball.

For Aristotle, the cricket ball's being heavier than the baseball is certainly not a substance. Is it an accident? Aristotle's accidents are dependent entities, like dents or wrinkles, they are modifications of substances, hence dependent on the substances they modify. Particular relations are likewise dependent on their relata. The heavier-than relation that obtains when a cricket ball is heavier than a particular baseball requires both the cricket ball and the baseball with their respective weights.

In this regard, relations resemble accidents. The identity of an accident depends on its bearer. If the heavier-than relation is an accident, then, what is its bearer? The bearer is not the cricket ball. If the baseball is destroyed, the relation would cease to be without affecting the cricket ball. Nor, for similar reasons, is the bearer the baseball. Could the bearer be *both* the cricket ball and the baseball? How could an accident belong to distinct entities? This is Leibniz's point in a much-cited passage in a letter to Samuel Clarke.

> The ratio or proportion of two lines L and M can be conceived in three ways: as a ratio of the greater L to the smaller M; as a ratio of the smaller M to the greater L; and lastly as something abstracted from both of them, that is to say as the ratio between L and M, without considering which is the anterior and which is the posterior, which the subject, which the object. In the first way of considering them, L the greater is the subject; in the second, M the smaller is the subject of this accident which philosophers call relation. But which will be the subject of the third way of considering them? We cannot say that the two, L and M together, are the subject of such an accident, for in that case we should have an accident in two subjects, with one leg in one and the other leg in the other, which is contrary to the notion of an accident. (Leibniz 1715: Fifth Paper, § 47)

Return to the dent in a car door. The dent is a particular modification of a particular door. This is not something that could be shared with or transferred to anything else. A dent partly in one door and partly in an adjacent panel is not a dent with a leg in both the door and the panel, but two dents, one in the door, one in the panel. Hammering the dent out of the panel leaves the dent in the door unaffected.

Take the cricket ball's bearing the heavier-than relation to the baseball. *Where* is this relation? It seems neither to be in the cricket ball, nor in the baseball. If you think of the relation as subsisting somehow *between* the two balls, you are thinking of it as a kind of substance. The idea is hard to credit. Substances, unlike accidents, are not dependent entities. The cricket ball's being heavier than the baseball, however, evidently depends on the respective weights of the cricket ball and the baseball.

One of the reviewers of this Element suggested that the question 'Where is the relation?' only seems odd in the case of internal relations. Returning to the cricket ball and baseball, the balls being a metre apart might be thought to reside, not in the balls, but in the space between them. I can understand the words, but not the thought they express. The relation is not a portion of air or a metre-long stretch of turf. It is invisible, intangible, and has all the marks of a posit of linguisticised metaphysics. Even if I were wrong about this, however, the relation's being located between the two balls means that it, the relation, stands in a relation to the balls, and Bradley's regress is back in play.

6.5 Relations as Sui Generis

If relations are neither substances nor accidents, what are they? I have already considered, and found wanting, the idea of replacing relations with relational properties, whether these are regarded as accidents (modes, tropes) or as universals (see Section 4.1). Aristotle and Leibniz both accept that, if relations are neither substances nor accidents, they are not entities.

This line of reasoning occurs again and again over the history of philosophical discussions of relations. Leibniz spoke for many when he observed: 'We are bound to say that the relation in this third way of considering it is indeed outside the subjects; but that being neither substance nor accident, it must be a purely ideal thing, the consideration of which is none the less useful' (Leibniz 1715: Fifth Paper, § 47). You might follow Russell and regard this as a *petitio principii*. At best, the argument establishes only that relations are neither substances nor accidents, not that relations are not real, not a kind of entity. Relations are *relations*, a distinct category of being.

Philosophers who make this response are wont to chastise those who profess puzzlement over the nature of relations or regard relations as 'odd' or 'weird' (MacBride 2020: § 2). Relations construed as substances or accidents would indeed be weird, but this is just the point. Relations are neither substances nor accidents. Relations are what answers to relational predicates. Given the indispensability of relational predicates, that we refer to and 'quantify over' relations, why not just accept relations as entities and be done with it? If this reinstates Bradley's regress, so be it.

By now you recognize that many philosophers have accepted this point and proceeded to offer solutions to Bradley's regress. This, however, elides the question, what is the nature of a relational entity? Relations are dependent on their relata. This is so even if you think of relations as universals: every instance of a relation would depend on its relata. A relation's holding between *a* and *b* requires *a* and *b*. In that case, although a given relation could fail to hold between *these* relata, it must hold between *some* relata – assuming that universals require instances.

In an effort to avoid unhelpful complexity, I propose to follow Locke in accepting that 'all things that exist are only particulars'. Properties, then, would be particulars – modes, accidents – not universals. If relations are entities, they too would be particulars. I do not think that this affects the points at issue and it has the advantage of allowing the discussion to flow without incessant qualifications concerning the metaphysics of properties. In any case, if you thought of relations as entities, then, if relations were universals, their particular instances would be the entities.

Given these ground rules, what can be said about the nature of relations? When a cricket ball is heavier that a particular baseball, what is this relation? (Strictly speaking, the relation holds between the balls only by courtesy, only because it holds between the balls' respective weights.) If relations are entities, they must have identity and persistence conditions: 'no entity without identity' (Quine 1969: 23). The heavier-than relation holding between *these* balls would not survive a change in the weight or the subtraction of either ball. The relation persists only so long as the balls do (with their respective weights).

Suppose the baseball were pulverized and replaced by another, precisely similar baseball. Would the relation survive? Not if it is a particular. As a particular, its holding requires these balls and these weights. Even if the relation were a universal, this instance would not survive, but would be supplanted by another instance.

The persistence and identity of a relation, then, is bound up with the persistence and identity of its relata. A relation persists so long as, and only so long as, its relata persist. What of the relation's *individuation* conditions? What makes it the case that this relation is the relation it is: a heavier-than relation holding between the respective weights of a particular cricket ball and a particular baseball? If you have these balls with these weights, you have its being true that the one is heavier than the other. For that, the respective weights of the balls suffices. But is there still an ontological commitment to a heavier-than relation?

Suppose God wants to create a cricket ball that is heavier than a particular baseball. It would seem that all God needs to do is create balls with these weights. Similarly, God's making it the case that one weight is heavier than another requires only that God create objects with these weights. The relation is on the scene because the respective weights are. That is what it *is* for these two weights – and by extension these two balls – to stand in the heavier-than relation. Why think that the relation is an additional piece of furniture? The ontological commitment here is to the balls and their respective weights.

This would seem to be the case for internal relations generally. If R is an internal relation, it is true both that 'a bears R to b' is made true by the existence of a and b, and that the judgement's ontological commitments do not go beyond the existence of a and b: a's bearing R to b is nothing more than a's being a and b's being b.

MacBride calls this 'reductionism about relations' (MacBride 2011: 165), but the kind of reduction in play is not analytic reduction. There is no suggestion that you could derive relational truths from non-relational truths or analyse or paraphrase talk of relations using a non-relational vocabulary. What, then, is being reduced to what? Are relations being reduced to properties? How would that work? How could something be reduced to something *else*? Or is reduction *elimination*? If relations are reduced to non-relations, would that mean that, after all, there really are no relations?

A better way to think about reduction here invokes truthmaking. In the case of internal relations, truthmakers for, and ontological commitments of, relational judgements include only propertied substances and no additional entities deserving to be called relations. Characterising this as reduction is potentially misleading, so I shall speak, instead, of the view that truthmakers for relational truths are non-relational features of the cosmos, with the understanding that this takes in the pertinent ontological commitments.

7 Relations and Non-relational Truthmakers

The possibility of there being relational truths with non-relational truthmakers might seem hopeless. How could '*aRb*' be *true*, if there is no *R*? Lacking an *R*, '*aRb*' would seem to be either false or meaningless. We ineliminably quantify over relations. How else could the widespread acceptance of relational truths as true be explained? Leibniz says that relations are 'purely ideal thing[s], the consideration of which is none the less useful' (Leibniz 1715: Fifth Paper, § 47). This suggests that talk of relations, like talk of the sun's rising and setting, while strictly false perhaps, is harmless enough and even conversationally required. When a friend remarks that the sun will rise tomorrow at 6:13 AM, it would be tiresomely pedantic to reply that, no, the sun does not rise, it only appears to rise because the Earth rotates on an axis at an angle of 23.5 degrees away from the plane of its elliptical orbit around the Sun.

The example dramatically understates the role played by relations in the sciences, however. Relations have an indispensable place in the theoretical framework of the sciences, and especially in physics. Some philosophers have taken this point to surprising ends, arguing that relations are all that is really out there. Talk of particles and their properties, for instance, is made true by relations. I shall return to this interesting thesis in Section 10. Meanwhile, it is worth noting that, whether or not relations are taken to be required as truthmakers for relational (and maybe non-relational) truths, they figure centrally in the sciences. Philosophers who find relations mysterious (or worse, unintelligible) would seem to be hopelessly out of touch.

Speaking now as an out of touch philosopher, I might offer a suggestion concerning arguments to the conclusion that the sciences are ontologically committed to relations. In various places I have inveighed against 'linguisticised metaphysics', a style of metaphysics in which forms of language call the shots. Thus, from the fact that we cannot but quantify over relations, the fact that equations we use to describe the finer interstices of nature are replete with relational terms, and the fact that the project of analysing away relations has proved hopeless, it is easy to conclude that a cosmos without relations could not be our cosmos. An absence of relations mandates an absence of relata. A cosmos that lacked relations would be a single, undifferentiated one, a prospect with pleasing mystical associations, but not one to be taken seriously. Right?

An instance of what I have in mind concerns the directionality or 'differential application' of non-symmetrical relations mentioned in Section 2.3. If Susan is Rebecca's mother, Rebecca is Susan's child. Are there two distinct relations here, the mother-of relation and the child-of relation? Or is there one state of the cosmos considered from two different perspectives? Leibniz, in a passage quoted earlier, uses the example of greater-than and smaller-than.

> The ratio or proportion of two lines L and M can be conceived in three ways: as a ratio of the greater L to the smaller M; as a ratio of the smaller M to the greater L; and lastly as something abstracted from both of them, that is to say as the ratio between L and M, without considering which is the anterior and which is the posterior, which the subject, which the object. (Leibniz 1715: Fifth Paper, § 47)

Considered apart from Rebecca and Susan, the relation they bear to one another is simply the mother–daughter relation. What makes it the case that Susan is Rebecca's mother (and Rebecca, Susan's daughter)? Unlike L and M, Rebecca and Susan's being as they are, intrinsically, is probably not sufficient. A molecule-for-molecule duplicate of Rebecca is not Susan's child. Susan must have given birth to Rebecca – another relation!

What makes it the case that Susan gives birth to Rebecca? You know the story: there is an embryo that matures and subsequently becomes an infant persisting on its own. Spelling out this description in more detail would require invoking countless relations, but the circumstances that make it the case that Susan is Rebecca's mother are not themselves relations. There are temporal befores and afters, spatial heres and theres, and causal bringings about. The situation could not be described without recourse to relational predicates, perhaps, but there is no room for relational entities accompanying whatever else is on the scene.

7.1 Spatial Relations

The discussion has been moving towards the idea that what makes it the case for things to stand in an internal relation is the relata's being as they are and nothing in addition. What of external relations? Consider spatial relations, paradigmatic – and maybe the *only* clear-cut instances of – external relations. Suppose you have two balls, a particular baseball and a companion cricket ball, and these are resting on the turf one metre apart. You could have these balls, just as they are intrinsically without their being a metre apart. If the balls are moving, the distance between them could be constantly changing.

Is that it, then? Must spatial relations be accepted as external, genuine ontological add-ons? Maybe not. Consider the balls' respective locations. The locations are where they are. The locations could not be anywhere else. Even if the fabric of space (or spacetime) bends and stretches, the locations do not move. You could think of space on the model of a chessboard. A chessboard comprises an eight-by-eight grid of squares, commonly labelled as in Figure 6.

Suppose the white king is on square g4. What makes it the case that square g4 is where *it* is? Where else *could* it be? You might stretch or distort the board in various ways, but the g4 square would remain what it is: the g4 square. What makes the g4 square the g4 square is its place in the space of squares. You might swap pieces of wood residing at g4 and b7, but that would not amount to swapping g4 and b7. Were you to move or distort the board, the g4 square would move relative to the board's external circumstances, but in the case of space (or spacetime), there are no external circumstances relative to which a location in space could move.

In putting it this way, I am not thinking of space (or spacetime, a qualification I shall henceforth assume) as made up of spatial points in the way a floor is made up of tiles. The tiles could be rearranged and retain their individual identities. A tile that was once here, is now over there. A floor made of tiles depends on the tiles that make it up. Space is not made up of points or regions. Points and regions of space are dependent for their identities on space, not it on them. In space so conceived, two locations a metre apart must be a metre apart. This would be so, even if space were stretched or crinkled. If the two balls are at *these* locations, they are thereby a metre apart.

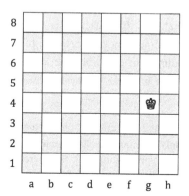

Figure 6 The layout of a chessboard

The relation between the locations is internal, perhaps, but what of the relation between the two balls, the occupants of the locations? The balls could have been at different locations, so why doubt that their being a metre apart is an external relation?

Start by asking yourself, what makes it the case that this ball is now at this location? This question should not be confused with the very different question, what *brought it about* that this ball is at this location? The ball might have been elsewhere, but at every point in its career, it must be somewhere. The ball must be at some location, and, for whatever reason, it is now at this location. The relation between the ball and its location at any given time is not, after all, an external relation (for further discussion, see Campbell 1990: ch. 5; Heil 2021: ch. 2).

Could this be right? You could have the ball and the ball's location, without the ball's being where it is, without the ball's being at this location. So the relation between the ball and its location must be external.

Well, the ball must be somewhere (and somewhen). What makes it the case that the ball is here, is that the ball is wherever it is, and where it is is here. This is going to be the case whatever the nature of space. Even if spatial locations were not essentially the locations they are, they are now the locations they are. If the balls are at these locations, and these locations are currently a metre apart, so are the balls. Spatial relations among objects in space are no additions of being.

7.2 Causal Relations

If you are still with me, I hope that you are prepared to move on and consider causal relations. If you think of causal relations as relations among events governed by contingent laws of nature, you are thinking of causal relations as external, something in addition to the relata. This is not the place to look at all the many approaches to causation, so I will paint with a broad brush, starting with the observation that, talk of causation is well suited to universes the occupants of which are distinct objects: particles, billiard balls, planets. This is the universe we encounter in everyday life and in scientific laboratories, Newton's universe, and the universe of classical mechanics. Keith Campbell puts it nicely:

> Thinking in terms of cause and effect is an essentially pluralistic way of conceptualising the universe. Cause and effect must be distinct existences for the notions to have any application at all. So discrete items (local events, specific instances of properties or particular objects), are the terms with which causation deals. Analysis, so often called for in refining a causal

explanation, identifies simpler and simpler structures as the protagonists in causal transactions, and so gives this inherent pluralism an atomistic tendency. (Campbell 1990: 124)

Currently, physics is pushing in the direction of a very different picture of the cosmos, one in which particles, billiard balls, and planets, are not mobile, self-contained clumps of matter, but distributions of energy in fields or thickenings of spacetime, or something stranger still. I shall say more about such cosmoses in Section 7.4. They have momentous implications for metaphysics generally, and, in particular, for the ontology of relations. For the present, I mean to focus on causation in a cosmos of particles and billiard balls as these are ordinarily conceived.

Imagine one billiard ball colliding with another and the subsequent alteration of the trajectories of both balls. Hume described such cases as ones in which you had an event – one ball's encountering another – followed by another – the balls changing their positions in a particular way. According to Hume, there is nothing more to an instance of causation, in particular, there is nothing about the balls that led them to behave as they did. Hume's idea was that when sequences similar to this one are common, we naturally come to expect similar outcomes in similar circumstances. We project our expectations onto nature, with the result that we seem to see causes bringing about or necessitating their effects, just as we seem to see objects on a television screen interacting.

This turns causal regularities into coincidences, something philosophers and scientists alike find repugnant. Science is in the business of discovering and, where possible, explaining natural regularities, and, in fact, many of these could be expressed mathematically in laws of nature. Laws, however, do not simply summarise coincidental regularities. Laws govern the behaviour of whatever falls under them.

What is it for a law to *govern* the behaviour of objects falling under it? Are laws entities that bring the objects to heel? That would be hard to swallow, but what are the options?

One option would be to invest the objects with powers or dispositions that, in concert with other powers, yield regular manifestations: objects' properties empower the objects in particular ways in concert with other variously empowered objects. Laws could then be seen as capturing, in a mathematically precise way, the contribution kinds of property make to objects they empower.

Mass and charge, for instance, properties of particles, might be thought to empower the particles in particular ways capturable by laws. Indeed, many philosophers have enthusiastically identified objects' properties with the powers of objects to affect and be affected by other empowered objects. As

Campbell observes, 'without powers, causation must remain mysterious, magical, and indeed occult' (Campbell 1990: 119).

7.3 Causation as the Manifesting of Powers

On such a conception, causation would be the manifesting of objects' powers. In the case of the billiard balls, you have one billiard ball (with a particular shape, mass, and momentum) striking a second billiard ball (with its own mass, shape, and momentum). Looking more closely, you have the first ball's striking the second, both balls compressing slightly, then rapidly decompressing with the result being the balls' subsequently move as they do.

Causation, thus construed, is *mutual* interaction (Heil 2012: ch. 6; Huemer and Kovitz 2003; Ingthorsson 2002). The interaction is simultaneous, not sequential. Think of a sugar cube's dissolving in a cup of hot tea. Powers belonging to the sugar and to the hot liquid work together to produce a dissolving. There is a before, when the sugar is deposited into the tea, and an after, sweetened tea, but the dissolving is simultaneous and continuous.

Although it is less obvious, this is so even in the billiard ball case. The balls interact as they do owing to their respective powers, but not just these. Powers belonging to the surface on which they rest, the enveloping atmosphere, and much else besides work together to yield a particular manifestation, a particular state of the cosmos. This state, in turn, in concert with other states, eventuates in new manifestations.

Seen in this light, the apparent asymmetry between causes and effects is an artefact of our interests. You might be interested in how to bring about something, or in what brought it about, or how to prevent something from occurring. Identifying something as the cause of a particular effect is strictly analogous to your identifying Susan as the mother of Rebecca or *L*'s being longer than *M*. You are thinking perspectively, considering a situation relative to Susan or to *L*. But the same situation could be described from the complementary perspective: Rebecca is Susan's daughter, *M* is shorter than *L*.

In the case of causation, you have one occurrence, the mutual manifesting of reciprocal powers, describable in two ways. In thinking of one billiard ball's striking another as the cause of the balls' trajectories changing, you are thinking of the first ball as responsible for the balls' new trajectories. But the balls' interaction is a cooperative affair requiring powers inherent in each ball to work together. If your interests were different, you might regard the second ball as the instigator, altering the course of the first ball.

This way of thinking about powers differs importantly from conceptions according to which powers are said to be triggered – or, worse, caused – so as to manifest themselves as they do (Bird 2007). If you have delved into recent work on powers (or dispositions), you have probably encountered philosophers who offer the following picture:

$$\text{stimulus} \rightarrow \text{power} \rightarrow \text{manifestation}$$

In contrast, the conception of powers on the table here is one in which powers combine forces so as to culminate in a manifestation.

$$\text{power} \rightarrow \text{manifestation} \leftarrow \text{power}$$

The emerging picture is of a massively interactive network of powers – what C. B. Martin calls a power net – that evolves over time, its state at any given time a manifestation of its state at earlier times (Martin 1997).

The identity of a power is determined by what it is a power *for*. A power is for particular kinds of manifestation in the company of particular kinds of reciprocal power. The upshot is a picture of the cosmos as a dynamic network of empowered objects that evolves as it does of necessity.

You might have doubts about this last claim, but it is a straightforward consequence of accepting that powers are individuated by what they are powers for – with particular kinds of reciprocal partner. If that is so, and if you have these powers in these arrangements, you have these manifestations.

Philosophers sometimes dispute this thought by noting that a power's manifestation can be 'blocked' or 'masked' even when it is in the company of reciprocal powers that, all together, would normally yield a particular kind of manifestation. Suppose, for instance, that a particular chemical would prevent or inhibit sugar's dissolving in hot liquids. If you lace a cup of hot tea with this chemical, then drop in a sugar cube, the sugar does not dissolve: its power to dissolve is blocked by the chemical. Indeed, you might arrange matters so that the very act of introducing sugar into the tea brings it about that the chemical is introduced, thereby 'finking' the dissolving. (Finks came on the scene with the 'Electro-Fink', a device introduced by Martin (1994: 2–4) as a counterexample to attempts to analyse talk of dispositions conditionally – 'as if–thens'.)

Describing something as a blocking, or masking, or finking, however, is to project our norms and expectations onto the situation. Sugar, together with ordinary hot tea, yields one sort of manifestation: sweetened tea. Sugar, in concert with hot tea and the imagined chemical yields a different sort of manifestation. The combination of sugar, hot tea, and the chemical manifests itself just as it must, given the nature of the powers at hand.

The same could be said of absences, lacks, and privations. A lack of water caused the plant to wilt. Does this mean that lacks are powers? Again, this thought is driven by pragmatic factors, not by the circumstances as they are. If you combine powers inherent in the plant and moist soil, you have one kind of manifestation: a thriving plant. In contrast, powers inherent in the plant and dry soil combine to yield another kind of manifestation: a struggling plant. Invoking the lack of water as a causal factor in the plant's wilting is to gild and stain the situation with our norms and expectations.

Thus characterised, a cosmos of interactive powers is ruthlessly deterministic. Physics tells us that some occurrences are not like this, however. When an unstable element – a radium atom, for instance – decays, its decaying when it does is unprompted. A radium atom has a half-life of about 1,600 years, that is, there is a probability of 50 per cent that the atom will decay sometime within its first 1,600 years. The atom's decay is uncaused, spontaneous. *How* the atom decays is fixed by its nature, but not *when* it decays. In effect, the atom has a power to manifest itself in a particular way on its own without the need for reciprocal powers.

This complicates the original story, but does not appreciably change it. The cosmos comprises a network of powers that evolves as it does because its occupants are empowered as they are. On the whole, its state at a particular time is necessitated by its state at an earlier time, although the occurrence of scattered spontaneous manifestations means that its state at any given time is affected by chancy occurrences. These could have momentous downstream consequences – think of the butterfly effect.

7.4 A Humean Alternative

This discussion of causation illustrates a signature feature of ontologically serious metaphysics: *one thing inevitably leads to another*. Once you are on the bus, you ride it to the end of the line where it comes to rest. You start with a simple billiard ball model of causation. This leads to an appeal to powers, and eventually you arrive at a cosmos of interacting objects that do whatever they do of necessity. In such a cosmos causation is no longer an external relation (if it ever was).

You could avoid this result by leaping off the bus mid-journey when you began to feel uncomfortable about where it was heading. You could also decide not to board the bus in the first place by not taking up powers in the course of explicating causation. This is the line adopted by Humeans such as David Lewis. (The philosopher, David Hume, might or might not have been a Humean in the style of Lewis.) In a Humean cosmos all you have is 'just one little thing and then another' (Lewis 1986a: ix). There is no give and take among distinct existences. Nothing interacts with or brings about anything else. Causal relations boil down to regularities, not a promising platform for anyone who regards causation as the engine of change.

Earlier, I observed that causation regarded as a kind of bringing about is tailored to a cosmos of distinct, interacting objects, but physics is increasingly casting doubt on the viability of this kind of cosmos. What we think of as objects – ultimately the particles, the quarks, leptons, muons – could turn out to be smeared-out concentrations of energy in fields, or maybe local thickenings in spacetime. The details are important, but for purposes of this discussion you need only imagine that the cosmos is a seamless field-like something. The particles are not grains of matter but concentrations of energy, the centres of which are local, but extend throughout the whole. What appear to us as interactions among particles and billiard ball-sized collections of particles are rather expressions of the nature of the whole. Changes in the configuration of particles stem, not from local interactions and manifestings, but from the whole's evolving as is its wont.

A cosmos of this kind would be Humean by virtue of its lack of interaction among distinct objects. What we think of as objects or substances would be accidents or, better, modes, relatively self-contained modifications of a seamless whole. What makes it the case that one billiard ball collides with another thereby affecting the trajectories of both, would be loosely analogous to a blush spreading across your face. The expansion of the blush is not due to local interactions among your skin cells; the blush wells up from forces inside you. The difference between the blush and what transpires in a seamless cosmos is that the blush is a manifestation of internal occurrences, while a seamless cosmos has no inside – nothing in the cosmos interacts with or affects anything else.

This is one way to understand Lewis's Humean cosmos as set out in the doctrine of 'Humean supervenience'.

> Humean supervenience is named in honor of the [great] denier of necessary connections. It is the doctrine that all there is to the world is a vast mosaic of local matters of particular fact, just one little thing after another. (But it is no part of the thesis that these local matters are mental.) We have geometry: a system of external relations of spatio-temporal distance between points. Maybe points of spacetime itself, maybe point-sized bits of matter or æther or fields, maybe both. And at these points we have local qualities: perfectly natural intrinsic properties which need nothing bigger than a point to be instantiated. For short: we have an arrangement of qualities. And that is all. There is no difference without difference in the arrangement of qualities. All else supervenes on that. (Lewis 1986a: ix–x)

I mention Lewis because his conception of how things stand has been criticised for failing to comport with the kind of physics I have been invoking. I am not so sure. Understood in a certain way, Lewis's cosmology is more nimble than his critics have supposed.

You can see what I mean by reflecting, first, on Lewis's comment that 'we have an arrangement of qualities. And that is all'. Is the cosmos, then, simply a collection of qualities? The qualities are distributed over spacetime, but what is spacetime? Another quality? A better option is suggested by Lewis himself. Suppose the qualities were not *in* spacetime, but *of* spacetime. The qualities would be modes, modifications of spacetime, not component parts adding up to the cosmos. Spacetime would lack parts, as well. It would have the character of a vast seamless substance modified locally – shades of Section 7! These modifications would not interact with one another, their dynamic character being an expression of the whole: Humeanism writ large.

I am not suggesting either that this is Lewis's view or that it should be embraced by physics. The point is just that this provides a serviceable model of a seamless cosmos and that this model is not obviously at odds with Humean supervenience.

In any case, this way of modelling Lewis's cosmology fits nicely with his embracing spacetime. Modifications of spacetime would neither interact nor come and go. Thinking of the cosmos as dynamic is to think of it at different times. Really it, the whole, simply is what it is. Causal interaction in such a cosmos would belong to the appearances. Causation features in the manifest image, but what makes it true, what makes it the case that colliding billiard balls affect one another's trajectories is, at bottom, a relatively compact four-dimensional pattern of qualities.

If you accept my earlier account of spatial relations as internal, and either a powers-based or Humean account of causation, then external relations begin to lose their sheen. There are relational truths, to be sure, but what makes it the case that these truths are true could be non-relational features of the cosmos.

8 Stocktake

Even if the status of external relations is threatened, this would not by itself knock out internal relations. My suggestion that ascriptions of internal relations are made true by their relata leaves unanswered MacBride's contention that we remain ontologically committed to relations – be they internal or external. Suppose that what makes it true that this cricket ball is heavier than that baseball is the balls' respective weights: if you have these weights, you have the relation. All God needs to do to get the relation on the scene is to create these balls with these weights. Even if this is so, it does not establish that the relation is not something in addition to the relata, only that the relation is on the scene of necessity (Section 6.1).

This brings us back to the nub of the difficulty in understanding the nature of relations. Suppose relations are something in addition to whatever they relate. What does the 'in addition to' signify? Leibniz holds that the addition is mental, not something 'out there' alongside the relata. In thinking that the weight of this ball is greater than that ball's weight, we are not considering a differential something, we are considering the balls differentially. When it comes to counting up entities on the scene, you have the balls with their respective weights, nothing more.

A relational entity would depend on its relata and, in that regard, have the status of a mode or accident. Relations hold between their relata, however, and, in that regard resemble substances. Given that relations are neither substances nor accidents, they must be sui generis, resembling Simons's relational tropes. Even if relations were universals, the entities on the scene would be instances, and these are hard to distinguish from tropes. The difference between tropes and instances of a universal is that exactly similar tropes, unlike instances of a universal, are numerically distinct.

In exploring the suggestion that relations are tropes, I focused on the question whether this would provide a way of avoiding Bradley's regress (Section 6.1). I sided with MacBride in concluding that the regress stems, not from the presumption that relations are universals, but from the presumption that they are entities. If relations are entities alongside their relata, they must be related to their relata.

Maybe the difference between a relation and a mode or an accident is that relations modify distinct substances – as Leibniz puts it, 'with one leg in one and the other leg in the other'. Leibniz adds that this is 'contrary to the notion of an accident', but, on the view under consideration, relations are relations, not accidents, and it is not obviously 'contrary to the notion' of a relation that it has a leg in distinct relata. So what would it be for a relation to modify or have a leg in each of its relata?

It would seem that the relata are fully what they are owing to their properties. If the relation ceases to be because one of the relata changes or itself ceases to be, its partner is constitutionally unaffected. We are back with the idea that the way relations depend on or modify their relata is sui generis. Why should this be considered a problem? It would be a problem if you thought that the aim of positing relational entities is explanatory. We have a sui generis species of entity that stands in a sui generis relation of dependence to its relata. This is close to the thought that relations relate because that is what they do. It beggars belief to think that ordinary and scientific talk of relations commits us to such entities.

Even if you were sanguine about positing entities the nature and function of which is opaque, however, you would still have to confront the 365 kilogram gorilla in the room: Bradley's regress. An instance of a relation or a relational trope stands in dependence relations to its relata. If these are relations and relations are entities, they would need to be on the scene if the original relation is to do its job. If proponents of relations as entities are right, then, even if the dependence relations between these new relations and the original relation were internal, as are their relations to the relata, that would not make them any less real than any other internal relation. For reasons canvassed in Section 6, the resulting regress is not benign. So long as relations are taken to be entities, they will need to be related to their relata in order to perform their function.

As is inevitable in any discussion of the ontology of relations, Bradley's views on the topic keep clambering for attention. I have hinted at those views and noted that they have often been misunderstood, but the discussion has reached the point at which discussion of them can no longer be postponed. With some trepidation, then, I now turn to Bradley the philosopher.

9 Bradley Redux

Before discussing Bradley's position, I am bound to interject a personal note. In a recent book, *Appearance in Reality*, I defended the thesis that, although relational truths are ineliminable, truthmakers for these truths could neverthe-less turn out to be non-relational features of the cosmos (Heil 2021). My title played off Bradley's *Appearance and Reality*, but I realised that I really had only a cursory understanding of what Bradley's position really was. As I was completing the book, it dawned on me that I needed to address Bradley directly, if only to say how my cosmology differed from his. I turned to Stewart Candlish's impressive work on Bradley, and I was stunned to learn that my position on relations and much else was in fact converging on Bradley's (see especially Candlish 1989 and 2007). At any rate, that is how it seemed to me. Although what follows owes much to Candlish, it reflects my own parochial understand-ing of Bradley.

A previously mentioned misconception of Bradley (see Section 6, especially Sections 6.1, and 6.2) concerns his attitude towards internal relations (see, for instance, Wollheim 1969). By and large, Bradley's critics interpret him as defending the claim that all relations are, at bottom, internal relations and subsequently arguing that, because internal relations are founded in their relata, there are no relations. Were that Bradley's considered position, it would suc-cumb to the kinds of difficulty addressed in the previous section: establishing that a relation is internal would not, by itself, establish its unreality.

Interpreting Bradley as holding that all relations are internal ignores a central feature of Bradley's position. The aim of the regress argument is to show that relations are unreal, not that 'they' are internal. Bradley's assumptions are shared by his critics. If relations were real, they would be entities. If they were entities, however, they would not be modes or accidents. Relations hold between, not of, their relata. In this regard, relations would have the character of substances, and, if relations were substances, they would stand in relations to their terms for reasons that by now should be familiar, and a regress ensues.

Bradley is by no means alone in accepting that something's being real amounts to its being a substance. If relations were real, then, they would be substances. But why think that? Why imagine that, if relations were real, they would perforce be substances? What about the trope option favoured by Simons? Tropes are not substances. Tropes are free-standing properties (or property instances). Thus conceived, tropes amount to what the scholastics and early moderns called real accidents: *real* because they existed apart from any substance, *accidents* because they were particular qualities, but not universals. Why not a category of real relations? This, in effect, is Simons's view.

Consider the red colour of a particular tomato. Were the tomato's colour a trope or real accident, it would be 'self-exemplifying': it would be red. Unless this were so, it would be mysterious how its inherence in the tomato could be responsible for the tomato's being red. A red trope would be a red something, a something that is the red way.

History has not been kind to real accidents. Many philosophers, including Descartes, doubted their intelligibility (Descartes 1641; see Heil 2012: 106–9, 2015a for discussion). They were not doubting that you could have something red, tomato-shaped and tomato-sized: a tomato would qualify. What they doubted was that any such entity would qualify as an accident. A red, roughly spherical something, or, for that matter, a red something, is a qualitied something, a substance. Armstrong makes this point about tropes and mentions A. J. Ayer who, in describing sense data, called them 'junior substances' (Armstrong 1989: 115; see also Robb 2005: 485–9).

The same points apply in spades to relational tropes or to any entity purporting to be a relation. Qualitative tropes would be qualitative somethings, but relations are neither qualities, nor qualitied. What are they, then? What is their nature? If all you can say about relational entities is that they are entities that relate, it would seem that relational entities are not nothings but not somethings either. Like real accidents, they are not just difficult, but impossible, to make out. As with so many philosophical gambits, you can grow comfortable talking the talk without having any clear notion of what you are talking about.

Ontologically serious metaphysics can expose, and thereby disarm, the pretence.

9.1 Bradley on Relations

Bradley's reservations about relations have merit. The ball is in the court of anyone who holds that relations are entities to which we are ontologically committed to the extent that we accept relational truths at face value. This is only the tip of the iceberg, however.

The belief, harboured by many of his critics, that Bradley held that relations are absorbed into their terms is not simply wrong, not simply misleading; it is deeply at odds with Bradley's larger picture. Suppose Bradley were right and there are no external relations. What would follow is not that all relations are internal, what Candlish calls the doctrine of internality, but that, without relations, there are no relata, no distinct objects to stand in relations. 'The doctrine of internality is an inherently unstable position. It is unstable because things that are internally related do not have – by definition – the kind of independence that is logically required of substances, and yet without such independence they cannot be thought of as related things at all' (Candlish 2007: 160).

You can appreciate Bradley's point by starting with a cosmos populated by distinct objects. If you have distinct objects, a dozen electrons, for instance, you have the electrons' standing in relations to one another. If external relations are unreal, then so are distinct relata. And, harkening back to Section 7, if there are no distinguishable objects to relate, there are no internal relations either.

What if Bradley were right and there are neither relations, nor objects to relate? Would that mean that relational judgements must be either false or meaningless? That would be hard to swallow given the role such judgements have in the sciences and in everyday life.

Bradley's contention is not that relational judgements are invariably false, but that talk of relations is tailored to the appearances, not to reality. We need relational language to negotiate the cosmos as we encounter it. There are innumerable relational truths. We must quantify over relations to say what we need to say in the sciences and in everyday life. This, in effect, is what Moore and Russell show. Relational predicates cannot be analysed away or eliminated in favour of non-relational predicates. This, however, leaves open the nature of what makes it the case that a relational judgement, when true, is true, what the appearances are appearances of: the cosmos that reveals itself to us in the guise of objects standing in relations includes neither distinct, relatable substances nor relations.

Relations and their relata would belong to the appearances, what Wilfrid Sellars calls the manifest image (Sellars 1962; Heil 2021). Bradley puts it this way: 'Mere internal relations, then, like relations that are merely external, are untenable if they make a claim to ultimate and absolute truth. But taken otherwise, and viewed as helpful makeshifts and as useful aids in the pursuit of knowledge, external and internal relations are both admissible and can be relatively real and true' (Bradley 1924: 645).

Bradley would likely want to distance himself from talk of truthmaking, but the point is just that our dependence on talk of relations leaves open the nature of what is the case when relational judgements – that Ben Nevis is taller than Sgùrr Alasdair – are true. The point is perfectly general. It is one thing to grasp the application conditions for a particular predicate, relational or otherwise, and to recognise when these have been satisfied, but it is another matter altogether to grasp the nature of whatever it is about reality that is responsible for reality's appearing as it does.

From Bradley's perspective, then, motivating a commitment to the reality of relations requires more than simply pointing to relational truths and their apparent ineliminability and concluding from these that relations must be real. The question remains: *do* relational truths require relational truthmakers or commit us ontologically to relations? Bradley offers reasons to doubt that they do.

9.2 Bradley's Monism

Bradley's attitude towards relations is of a piece with his advocacy of monism, the view that there is exactly one substance, the Absolute. This topic remained in the background during Bradley's ongoing debate with Russell over relations, but, for Bradley, relations and pluralism about substances must stand or fall together. If relations are unreal, pluralism is false, and we have better reasons for denying the reality of relations than we have for affirming pluralism. From this perspective, Russell's advocacy of logical atomism undermines itself.

> The Russell of 1918 reminds us that each of his particulars 'stands entirely on its own and is completely self-subsistent', having 'that sort of self-subsistence that used to belong to substance', so that 'each particular that there is in the world does not in any way logically depend upon any other particular' (Russell 1918: 179). There are, broadly speaking, two ways in which such independence can be achieved. One is Russell's logical atomist way: extrude complexity from objects into facts, so that the complexes lose their status as objects and the substances are independent in virtue of their simplicity. Another is Bradley's: absorb complexity so that the eventual sole substance has its independence in virtue of there being nothing else. (There

are, of course, also attempts to have it both ways, such as Leibniz's.) But the
point is that what systems of both kinds agree on is that internal relations not
only are unreal themselves because all relations are, but also undermine the
reality of their terms, even if not everyone would like this idealist way of
putting it. (Candlish 2007: 160)

Monism is currently enjoying a resurgence in metaphysical circles, in part
owing to pressures from physics. As noted earlier (Sections 7.2 and 7.4), what
we regard as particles – quarks, leptons, muons – could, for all we know, turn
out to be disturbances in fields, or in a single, unified field, or thickenings in
space or spacetime. Were that the case, what we regard as distinct objects would
turn out not to be substances, but to be modes or accidents. Modes and accidents
are dependent entities incapable of existing apart from the substance they
modify. Because they are not substances, but modifications of a substance,
they would not count as real for Bradley. They would not themselves be entities.

The point is worth reemphasising. When Bradley declares that something is
not real, he means that the something is not a substance. If something, the tree in
the quad, is unreal, the tree is not a substance. That would be so were the tree
a mode, a local modification of the Absolute. The tree's being unreal does not
yield the result that judgements concerning the tree are false or misguided, or
that the tree is an illusion. The appearances do not stand as a veil between us and
reality. Reality is what the appearances are appearances of, but you cannot
extract the nature of reality directly from the appearances, directly from the
ways it appears to us.

> The question always lurking more or less visibly behind Bradley's arguments
> is, 'Are relations and their terms real?' I have said already that this question is
> the same as, 'are relations and their terms substances?' and that the linguistic
> counterpart of this question, for him at least, is 'Do names of relations and
> their terms figure in a language which accurately mirrors reality?'. (Candlish
> 2007: 167)

Bradley offers a priori arguments for monism. Physics could be seen as
offering complementary a posteriori arguments tending towards a similar conclusion. Particles, regarded as substances distributed in space, could give way to
fields or spacetime, a possibility with distinctly Bradleyan overtones.

By way of illustration, imagine that there is a single substance, spacetime,
a stand-in for the Absolute, and that what we regard as objects are local thickenings or modifications of this substance. The modifications are fully particular, not
universals. Their character is illuminated by an example deployed previously.
A mode is akin to a dent in a car door. The dent is a particular modification of the
door. The dent owes its identity to the door. This dent could not be moved to

another door or, for that matter, to another location on the door it modifies. The door could have been differently dented, perhaps, but the dent could not have been other than it is. For Bradley, modes would not count as real, but, again, this is to say no more than that modes are not substances. Modes are dependent on substances. For a dent to be on the scene, you need something to be dented.

The possibility that what we commonly regard as particles and objects made up of particles belong to the appearances, not to reality would be congenial to Bradley. It could as well be congenial to physics, and in particular, quantum physics. Newtonian physics and quantum physics are both committed to what appears to be action at a distance. Newtonian gravitational attraction is instantaneous and universal. The motion of every particle immediately affects and is affected by the motions of all the others, however remote. Although gravitational forces diminish over distance, they are never entirely absent. In the case of quantum physics, particles in entangled states exhibit 'non-locality'. Despite the absence of an intervening physical connection, a measurement here affords evidence for a result over there.

In neither case are observed correlations among the particles explicable causally. A measurement or the movement of a particle here does not, and in fact could not, instantaneously bring about something over there. Rather, the system to which the particles belong evolves in a way that issues in coordination among distinct states. Although changes here reflect changes elsewhere, these are correlations stemming from the nature of the whole, not instances of genuine action at a distance.

In a Bradleyan cosmos in which particles are modes, modifications of spacetime, for instance, there are no interactions among substantial particulars, and certainly no action at a distance. Instead, the whole evolves as it does because that is its nature, because the whole is what it is. Observable correlations would not be explained causally. They would be localised expressions of the whole.

All this is highly speculative, but my aim has not been to advance an interpretation of quantum physics, but merely to suggest that Bradley's approach to relations and substances is not obviously at odds with physics, and might well be better suited than its pluralistic competitors to accommodate phenomena such as quantum entanglement. Again, one thing has led to another to issue in an apparently surprising outcome.

9.3 A Loose End

You might have reservations about all this, indeed, it would be surprising if you did not. I have painted Bradley in a distinctly favourable light, repeatedly giving him the benefit of the doubt. But even someone sympathetic to Bradley's holistic picture might resist the idea that relations are unreal. After all, even if the tree and the quad are modifications of the Absolute, they nevertheless stand in relations to one another and to many other objects-cum-modifications as well. The tree is in the quad, the quad is in the university. Why should replacing substances with modes strike relations from the scene?

In response, two points bear mention. First, relations are fully present in the appearances, upstanding citizens of the manifest image. They are absent only in what Sellars calls the scientific image and Bradley calls reality. I have encouraged the Bradleyan thought that truthmakers for truths concerning the manifest image belong to the cosmos depicted by the scientific image, Bradley's Absolute.

Second, you might still worry that, the manifest image aside, if the Absolute is a mottled one, relations among the mottles – mottles being modes – are retained. The relations would not hold between substances, but why should that matter? Dents in a car door can stand in various relations to one another.

Notice that, in Bradley's cosmology, as in its Humean counterpart discussed in Section 7.4, everything is as it is essentially, including the whole. Just as a dent or a wrinkle, could not have been other than it is, so a cosmos of dents and wrinkles could not have been other than it is. Any differences would belong to a distinct cosmos, and it is, at the very least, an open question whether there could have been a different cosmos. Contingency, which philosophers profess to see everywhere, is in the eye of the beholder.

To think about or describe such a cosmos, you need relational concepts and a relational vocabulary. This is a manifestation of our finitude, however, not a reflection of reality. We are not equipped to take in the whole at once, so we make do with abstraction, what Locke called partial consideration, addressing the cosmos partially and knitting together partial glimpses into a complex whole that constitutes the manifest image, Bradley's appearances.

Reality is what appears. The appearances are suggestive but unreliable guides to the nature of what appears, the nature of reality. If this strikes you as excessive, ask yourself how reliable the appearances are when it comes to the cosmos as characterised by quantum physics or general relativity.

The appearances are awash with relations in the sense that they reflect our limited access to what there is. This does not mean, however, that the appearances include elements standing in relations. The appearances are not sense data or mental representations. The appearances are just reality as we encounter it: partially and from a finite, parochial perspective.

10 Relational Ontology

Bradley's account of the symbiosis between relations and substantial pluralism affords a convenient transition to a very different approach to relations, one that puts relations in the driver's seat. The idea, very roughly, is that there is nothing more to a particle – or any substantial entity – than relations it bears to other particles. Randall Dipert provides an excellent early statement of a position of this kind (Dipert 1997). Dipert speaks of 'the mathematical structure of the world', but, more recently, 'ontic structural realists' have proposed a relational ontology aimed at the unification of quantum physics and general relativity (Esfeld 2016, 2020; Ladyman et al. 2007).

Although I am out of my depth in discussing quantum physics, I can at least give you a feel for the position as it is articulated by Michael Esfeld (to whom I apologise in advance). Esfeld begins with the kinds of 'non-locality' consideration introduced in the previous section. Start with the idea that the cosmos comprises a dynamic arrangement of particles. A particle's trajectory through spacetime cannot be understood in isolation from the trajectories of other particles. An observation of an occurrence here can afford evidence for an occurrence over there. There is no question of the one's causing the other. The whole system of particles evolves in a way that suggests coordination among the particles, rather as if every particle were aware of the movements of every other particle and adjusted its own movements accordingly.

How might this work? Esfeld depicts the cosmos as comprising insensible 'point particles' that lack any intrinsic nature. The character of a particle is exhausted by its spatio-temporal location relative to every other particle. A proton's being positively charged and an electron's being negatively charged are not intrinsic, empowering features of the proton and electron. What makes it the case that a particle is positively or negatively charged is its favouring one sort of trajectory relative to the trajectories of its fellow particles rather than another.

On this view, point particles are not Newtonian atoms, not impenetrable, indivisible, insensible mobile bits of matter scurrying about in space. A particle is constituted by relations it bears to other particles, and space or spacetime is the particles standing in these relations. Particles are distinguished from one another by their relative locations over time. A particle's identity, its being the particle it is and its being the kind of a particle it is, is determined, not by its intrinsic nature – it has none – but by its spacetime trajectory. Only the configuration of particles has what might deserve to be called an intrinsic nature. The configuration is not a configuration of *it*s, the only *it* is the configuration.

Particles so conceived are not self-subsistent, hence not substances. God's creating a new particle would not be a local punctate affair. Bringing a particle into existence would require retuning the whole configuration in a particular way.

10.1 Where's the Beef?

Esfeld's holistic picture has affinities with Bradley's Absolute. Esfeld's cosmos is a whole, but not a whole made up of parts standing in relations to one another. The 'parts' – the particles – are abstractions from the whole, the whole considered in a particular way. The difference between Esfeld and Bradley turns on the role played by relations for Esfeld. Esfeld's whole is constituted by relations, a conception at odds with Bradley's in at least two respects.

First, Bradley holds that if relations are real they must be substances, and it is unlikely that Esfeld's relations could be regarded as substances. One motivation for embracing a cosmos of relations is to turn substances – the particles – into virtual entities subject to global constraints. Second, and more significantly, for Bradley relations require substantial relata (and substantial entities, in turn, stand in relations). In dispensing with relations, Bradley takes himself to have dispensed with a plurality of substances as well. Thus, despite intriguing formal similarities, Bradley's cosmos and Esfeld's relational alternative are evidently deeply at odds.

Bradley aside, what is there to be said for a cosmology of relations in which relata are constituted by relations they bear to other relata? Such an cosmology is reminiscent of one proposed by Roger Boscovich in the eighteenth century as a competitor to Newton's (Boscovich 1763; see Campbell 1976, ch. 6 for discussion). Newton's cosmos was populated by indivisible impenetrable atoms and assemblages of atoms that exerted forces on one another proportional to their masses and inversely proportional to the square of their distances from one another. Boscovich replaced Newton's atoms with extensionless point particles that, like Esfeld's particles, lacked intrinsic natures. A material point is a locus of accelerative forces and nothing more. Boscovich's material points 'affect the velocities of all others in a single standard fashion which depends only on the distance between them. The effects produced are accelerations. They are either attractive or repulsive depending on the distance separating the points' (Campbell 1976: 86).

Unlike Esfeld's point particles, Boscovich's particles are characterised by accelerative forces. The trajectories of Esfeld's particles are not brought about by particles' exercising powers and exerting forces on one another. In Esfeld's cosmos, there are no forces, no causal interactions among particles. Particle trajectories are expressions of holistic constraints on particle motions. For Boscovich, the nature of a particle is exhausted by its interactions with other particles, the nature of which is likewise exhausted by interactions with other particles. In contrast, the nature of an Esfeld point particle is exhausted by its location over time relative to other particles, the nature of which is similarly exhausted by their locations over time relative to other particles.

These differences are significant, but they mask an important similarity. Esfeld and Boscovich both envisage cosmoses in which a particle is a something the character of which is exhausted by its relations to other somethings, the character of which, in turn, is exhausted by their relations to other relationally charactered somethings, including the original something. Are such cosmoses intelligible? Maybe not. Campbell, addressing Boscovich, asks

> What are material points made of? They are not made of anything. They do not have any intrinsic features, like mass, or hardness, or solidity, or shape, or size in virtue of which we could give them a nature. Their only feature, other than location, is that they accelerate other points. (Campbell 1976: 93)

What, then, *are* material points?

> What distinguishes a location in space where there is a point from one where there is no such thing? All we can say is: At a material point there is something which accelerates other somethings which in turn accelerate somethings (including the first) which in turn …. But what an odd object this is; its only feature is to have an effect on things which have an effect on things which have an effect on things which … We seem to be caught in a regress or circle, forever unable to say just what these things are which have an effect on each other. (Campbell 1976: 93)

How are we to understand *what* is affecting and being affected? The protagonist in a 1980's Wendy's commercial sums it up succinctly: 'Where's the beef?'.

10.2 Not Nothings but Not Somethings Either

Proponents of relational ontologies might object to this line of criticism for reasons not unlike those offered by philosophers in defending the reality of relations generally. Addressing an ontology in which there are no somethings standing in relations, only relations, it would be question-begging to insist that related somethings must have intrinsic qualitative natures. Physics has no use for qualitative natures in explaining the behaviour of particles, so why not dispense with them once and for all? Why countenance intrinsic qualitative natures if they contribute nothing to the insensibles?

First, Bradley's point: relations stand or fall with a pluralism of substances. Either without the other is unintelligible. Relations require relata, relata relations. Second, like Campbell, you might find a purely relational ontology, one in which relata are constituted by relations hopelessly *recherché*. Boscovich and Esfeld set the table with an ontology of particles standing in spatial locations, then subtract the particles because physics is said to be concerned only with the relations among particles. The difficulty is to get a grip on the ontology of a cosmos comprising somethings constituted by relations among nothings. Suppose you start with a's bearing R to b – a is next to b, for instance. Now subtract a and b, and do so without subtracting R. A neat trick if you can bring it off.

Richard Holton envisages a cosmos, W_R, comprising four objects, A, B, C, and D (Holton 1999). These are said to be wholly constituted by relations they bear to one another:

A is directly to the left of B and directly above C.
B is directly to the right of A, and directly above D.
C is directly to the left of D, and directly below A.
D is directly to the right of C, and directly below B.

You could represent W_R by means of a diagram (Figure 7).

The labelled dots are meant only as aids to our visualising W_R. As Holton puts it, 'there really is nothing more to A, B, C, and D than that given by the descriptions' (Holton 1999: 10). You move from a representation of W_R to W_R itself by erasing the dots, leaving behind the relations. If the relations survive, would this be enough to leave the original relata (as represented by the dots) intact? Are their still somethings at or between these dots – or anywhere else in W_R?

More likely this a case in which you move from the relatively uncontroversial claim that you could give a purely relational representation of an imagined cosmos (adopting Dipert's recommendation to use graph theory, for instance) to the much stronger claim that this is all there is to the cosmos thus described.

Such a move is especially attractive to philosophers who start with scientific formalisms and proceed to extract an ontology directly from these. The result,

A • B •

C • D •

Figure 7 A purely relational cosmos

fully implemented, issues in Pythagoreanism: the cosmos as number (Martin 1997). Are you prepared to go there?

A second reason for doubting the viability of a purely relational cosmos is less exciting but no less pressing. Physics abstracts from objects' qualities in explaining their behaviour, but it would be a mistake to conclude from this that the objects lack qualities. We invariably engage in abstraction – Locke's partial consideration – in thinking about and explaining ordinary goings-on. You abstract from a billiard ball's colour when you explain why it rolls, rather than bounces or slides across a billiard table, but this does not mean that the ball lacks a colour, much less that it altogether lacks a qualitative nature. Your not seeing the dog barking beneath your window is not your perceiving a canine absence, and it is certainly not grounds for concluding that the dog is an unmotivated posit: all you need is the bark. Robert Musil's 'Man without Qualities' is not literally a man without qualities.

For my part, I struggle to comprehend how qualitied somethings – billiard balls, rabbits, pointers on an instrument that detects the motions of insensible particles – could be made up of mobile unqualitied nothings? This is not simply another version of the Hard Problem; it is not about conscious experiences, it is about qualitatively imbued objects 'out there'. You might do what many others have done, and relegate these to the mind, but in so doing you place minds apart from the cosmos. Is there any reason to doubt that, if there are insensible particles, these have qualitative natures? Our commerce with the insensibles depends on their effects on instruments built to detect them, but this does not mean that the nature of an insensible is exhausted by its relations to other insensibles, including those that make up detectors.

Finally, I cannot resist observing that Bradley's cosmos, competently developed, could turn out to afford a less fraught and more satisfying basis for the unification of quantum physics and general relativity than a purely relational counterpart. I am not equipped to make good on this suggestion, but it does seem to me that appeals to qualitatively bereft, purely relational cosmoses set a low bar for improvement.

11 Relations: Can't Live with 'Em, Can't Live without 'Em

This Element began by asking why philosophers disagree so sharply over the nature of relations and even over whether there *are* any relations? Philosophers are regularly accused of raising questions about what no one else doubts then disagreeing fiercely on how the questions should be answered. When scientists find themselves with disagreements of this kind, disagreements that cannot be settled experimentally, they conclude that they have been barking up the wrong tree. Why are philosophers so stubborn, so unwilling to see when a project is hopeless and move on?

This attitude towards philosophy is convenient, even necessary, if the sciences are to make progress, but it belies an important truth. Philosophy, or at any rate metaphysics, is inevitable. Metaphysical questions arise spontaneously without antecedent philosophical prompting. Non-philosophers can get away with repressing the questions or dismissing them as 'merely philosophical'. The upshot: philosophers are left with the questions no one else wants to address, then upbraided for not producing easily digestible, uncontroversial answers.

In the case of relations, the metaphysics starts to matter when philosophers step up and offer to assist physicists in providing an ontology for quantum physics founded on relations. The worry is not that the ontology might send physicists down the wrong path; the philosophers, after all, are following the physicists. The worry, rather, is that the business of providing interpretations of theoretical formalisms goes beyond the theories and evidence supporting those theories and shades into metaphysics. A formally consistent but metaphysically dodgy ontology threatens to foreclose the search for more respectable alternatives.

The aim of the sciences is not merely to provide reliable vehicles for predictions and interventions. We would also like to understand what the cosmos would be like if those theories are true. Quantum physics gives us an elegant and reliable theoretical structure. But quantum physics continues to be frustrating, even to physicists, because it remains unclear what a cosmos in which the theory holds true would be like. Under the circumstances, the question whether a purely relational cosmos is metaphysically viable forces itself on us and leads inevitably to thoughts about the nature of relations.

You have made it to the end: congratulations! If I have accomplished nothing else, I hope that I have at least brought you to see that the philosophical endeavour to come to grips with the status and character of relations is not an idle pastime pursued exclusively by academic ratbags who lack the brains or the courage to pursue issues that really matter. Questions about the nature of relations spring directly from our ongoing engagement with the cosmos and force themselves on us whether we like it or not. Self-consciously turning your back on these questions or writing them off as merely philosophical would amount to an exhibition of bad faith.

Go well.

References

Armstrong, D. M. 1989 *Universals: An Opinionated Introduction*. Boulder, CO: Westview Press.

Armstrong, D. M. 1997 *A World of States of Affairs*. Cambridge: Cambridge University Press.

Armstrong, D. M. 2004 *Truth and Truthmakers*. Cambridge: Cambridge University Press.

Bigelow, J. 1988 *The Reality of Numbers: A Physicalist's Philosophy of Mathematics*. Oxford: Clarendon Press.

Bird, A. 2007 *Nature's Metaphysics: Laws and Properties*. Oxford: Clarendon Press.

Boscovich, R. J. 1763 [1966] *A Theory of Natural Philosophy*, trans. J. M. Child. Cambridge, MA: MIT Press.

Bradley, F. H. 1893 *Appearance and Reality*. London: Swan Sonnenschein. Corrected edition, Oxford: Clarendon Press, 1930.

Bradley, F. H. 1924 'Relations'. Published posthumously in F. H. Bradley, *Collected Essays*. Oxford: Clarendon Press, 1935: 629–76.

Cameron, R. P. 2010 'Necessity and Triviality'. *Australasian Journal of Philosophy* 88: 401–15.

Campbell, K. 1976 *Metaphysics: An Introduction*. Encino, CA: Dickenson Publishing Co.

Campbell, K. 1990 *Abstract Particulars*. Oxford: Basil Blackwell.

Candlish, S. 1989 'The Truth about F. H. Bradley'. *Mind* 98: 331–48.

Candlish, S. 2007 *The Russell/Bradley Dispute and Its Significance for Twentieth-Century Philosophy*. Basingstoke, UK: Palgrave Macmillan.

Candlish, S. and P. Basile 2017 'Francis Herbert Bradley'. *The Stanford Encyclopedia of Philosophy* (Spring 2017 Edition), ed. Edward N. Zalta. https://plato.stanford.edu/archives/spr2017/entries/bradley/.

Cook, J. W. 1968 'Hume's Scepticism with Regard to the Senses'. *American Philosophical Quarterly* 5: 1–17.

Davidson, D. 1970 'Mental Events'. In L. Foster and J. Swanson, eds., *Experience and Theory*. Amherst, MA: University of Massachusetts Press: 79–101. Reprinted in *Essays on Actions and Events*. Oxford: Clarendon Press, 1980: 207–25; and in J. Heil, ed., *Philosophy of Mind: A Guide and Anthology*. Oxford: Oxford University Press, 2003: 685–99.

Descartes, R. 1641 *Fourth Set of Replies: Reply to Points Which May Cause Difficulty to Theologians*. In J. Cottingham, R. Stoothoff, and D. Murdoch, trans., *The Philosophical Writings of Descartes*, vol. 2. Cambridge: Cambridge University Press, 1984: 172–8.

Dipert, R. R. 1997 'The Mathematical Structure of the World: The World as Graph'. *Journal of Philosophy* 94: 329–58.

Esfeld, M. 2016 'The Reality of Relations: The Case from Quantum Physics'. In A. Marmodoro and D. Yates, eds., *The Metaphysics of Relations*. Oxford: Oxford University Press: 218–34.

Esfeld, M. 2020 *Science and Human Freedom*. London: Palgrave Macmillan.

Hare, R. M. 1952 *The Language of Morals*. Oxford: Oxford University Press.

Heil, J. 2000 'Truth Making and Entailment'. *Logique et Analyse* 169–70: 231–42.

Heil, J. 2003 *From an Ontological Point of View*. Oxford: Clarendon Press.

Heil, J. 2006 'The Legacy of Linguisticism'. *Australasian Journal of Philosophy* 84: 233–44.

Heil, J. 2009 'Relations'. In R. Le Poidevin and R. Cameron, eds., *Routledge Companion to Metaphysics*. London: Routledge: 310–21.

Heil, J. 2012 *The Cosmos as We Find It*. Oxford: Clarendon Press.

Heil, J. 2015a 'Cartesian Transubstantiation'. In J. Kvanvig, ed., *Oxford Studies in the Philosophy of Religion*, vol. 6. Oxford: Oxford University Press: 139–57.

Heil, J. 2015b 'Relations'. In F. Clementz and J.-M. Monnoyer, eds., *The Metaphysics of Relations*. Frankfurt: Ontos Verlag: 310–21.

Heil, J. 2021 *Appearance in Reality*. Oxford: Clarendon Press.

Holton, R. 1999 'Dispositions All the Way Round'. *Analysis* 59: 9–14.

Huemer, M. and B. Kovitz. 2003 'Causation as Simultaneous and Continuous'. *The Philosophical Quarterly* 53: 556–65.

Hume, D. 1788 *A Treatise of Human Nature*, eds., D. F. Norton and M. J. Norton. Oxford: Oxford University Press, 2001.

Ingthorsson, R. D. 2002 'Causal Production as Interaction'. *Metaphysica* 3: 87–119.

Keinänen, M. and T. E. Tahko. 2019 'Bundle Theory with Kinds'. *The Philosophical Quarterly* 69: 838–57.

Kim, J. 1990 'Supervenience as a Philosophical Concept'. *Metaphilosophy* 12: 1–27. Reprinted in J. Kim, *Supervenience and Mind: Selected Philosophical Essays*. Cambridge: Cambridge University Press, 1993: 131–60.

Ladyman, J. and D. Ross, with D. Spurrett and J. Collier. 2007 *Every Thing Must Go: Metaphysics Naturalized*. Oxford: Oxford University Press.

Leibniz, G. W. 1715 'Leibniz–Clarke Correspondence', trans. M. Morris and G. H. R. Parkinson. In G. H. R. Parkinson, ed., *Leibniz: Philosophical Writings*. London: J. M. Dent & Sons, 1973.

Lewis, D. K. 1986a *Philosophical Papers*, vol. 2. New York: Oxford University Press.

Lewis, D. K. 1986b *On the Plurality of Worlds*. Oxford: Basil Blackwell.

Lewis, D. K. 2001 'Truthmaking and Difference-Making'. *Noûs* 35: 602–15.

Locke, J. 1690 *An Essay Concerning Human Understanding*, ed., P. H. Nidditch. Oxford: Clarendon Press, 1978.

MacBride, F. 2005 'The Particular–Universal Distinction: A Dogma of Metaphysic'. *Mind* 114: 565–614.

MacBride, F. 2011 'Relations and Truthmaking'. *Proceedings of the Aristotelian Society* 111: 161–79.

MacBride, F. 2020 'Relations'. *Stanford Encyclopedia of Philosophy*, ed., E. N. Zalta. https://plato.stanford.edu/archives/win2020/entries/relations/.

McKeon, R., ed. 1941 *The Basic Works of Aristotle*. New York: Random House.

McTaggart, J. M. E. 1921 *The Nature of Existence*, vol. 1. Cambridge: Cambridge University Press.

Martin, C. B. 1980 'Substance Substantiated'. *Australasian Journal of Philosophy* 58: 3–10.

Martin, C. B. 1994 'Dispositions and Conditionals'. *The Philosophical Quarterly* 44: 1–8.

Martin, C. B. 1997 'On the Need for Properties: The Road to Pythagoreanism and Back'. *Synthese* 112: 193–231.

Martin, C. B. 2008 *The Mind in Nature*. Oxford: Clarendon Press.

Maurin, A.-S. in press *Properties (Cambridge Elements in Metaphysics)*. Cambridge: Cambridge University Press.

Moore, G. E. 1919 'External and Internal Relations'. *Proceedings of the Aristotelian Society* 20: 40–62.

Perovic, K. in press *Ontological Categories (Cambridge Elements in Metaphysics)*. Cambridge: Cambridge University Press.

Quine, W. V. O. 1969 *Ontological Relativity and Other Essays*. New York: Columbia University Press.

Rayo, A. 2010 'Towards a Trivialist Account of Mathematics'. In O. Bueno and O. Linnebo, eds., *New Waves in Philosophy of Mathematics*. Basingstoke, UK: Palgrave Macmillan: 239–62.

Robb, D. M. 2005 'Qualitative Unity and the Bundle Theory'. *The Monist* 88: 466–92.

Russell, B. 1903 *The Principles of Mathematics*. London: Allen & Unwin, 1937.

Russell, B. 1910 *Philosophical Essays*. London: Longmans, Green, and Co. Republished, New York: Simon and Schuster, 1966.

Russell, B. 1918 'The Philosophy of Logical Atomism'. In D. Pears, ed., *The Philosophy of Logical Atomism*. La Salle, IL: Open Court Publishing Co. 1985: 35–155.

Sellars, W. 1962 'Philosophy and the Scientific Image of Man'. In R. Colodny, ed., *Frontiers of Science and Philosophy*. Pittsburgh, PA: University of Pittsburgh Press: 35–78. Reprinted in W. Sellars, *Science, Perception, and Reality*. London: Routledge and Kegan Paul, 1963: 1–40.

Simons, P. 2010 'Relations and Truthmaking'. *Proceedings of the Aristotelian Society* 84(supplementary volume): 199–213.

Wieland, J. W. and A. Betti. 2008 'Relata-Specific Relations: A Response to Vallicella'. *Dialectica* 62: 509–24.

Williams, D. C. 1953 'On the Elements of Being'. *Review of Metaphysics* 7: 3–18; 171–92. Reprinted as 'The Elements of Being' in D. C. Williams, *Principles of Empirical Realism*. Springfield, MO: Charles C. Thomas, 1966: 74–109; and in A. R. J. Fisher ed., *The Elements and Patterns of Being*. Oxford: Oxford University Press: 2018: 24–50.

Wollheim, R. 1969 *F. H. Bradley*. Revised ed. Harmondsworth, UK: Penguin.

Acknowledgements

Many people have influenced my thoughts on relations, including six friends and philosophers no longer in our midst: David Armstrong, Donald Davidson, Jonathan Lowe, Charlie Martin, Hugh Mellor, and Jack Smart. I have tried to give credit where it is due in the preceding pages, but I am sure I have left out many others who deserve mention. I am indebted to Tuomas Tahko who, in inviting me to contribute to the Cambridge Elements in Metaphysics series, gave me the chance to reflect seriously on relations and make choate what had previously been inchoate in my thoughts on the topic. Some of those inchoate thoughts appear in 'Relations' (in R. Le Poidevin and R. Cameron, eds., *Routledge Companion to Metaphysics*, London: Routledge, 2009: 310–21; and in F. Clementz and J.-M. Monnoyer, eds., *The Metaphysics of Relations*, Frankfurt: Ontos Verlag, 2015: 310–21). Tuomas, together with Anne Elliott-Day and two anonymous readers for Cambridge University Press, did their best to keep me honest and save me from myself by providing innumerable corrections and suggestions that improved the Element substantially. Most of all, I am grateful both for and to Harrison Hagan Heil. Her love, wisdom, and clear-headed mastery of well-tempered prose enabled me to persevere.

Cambridge Elements ☰

Metaphysics

Tuomas E. Tahko

University of Bristol

Tuomas E. Tahko is Professor of Metaphysics of Science at the University of Bristol, UK. Tahko specializes in contemporary analytic metaphysics, with an emphasis on methodological and epistemic issues: 'meta-metaphysics'. He also works at the interface of metaphysics and philosophy of science: 'metaphysics of science'. Tahko is the author of *Unity of Science* (CUP, 2021, *Elements in Philosophy of Science*), *An Introduction to Metametaphysics* (CUP, 2015) and editor of *Contemporary Aristotelian Metaphysics* (CUP, 2012).

About the Series

This highly accessible series of Elements provides brief but comprehensive introductions to the most central topics in metaphysics. Many of the Elements also go into considerable depth, so the series will appeal to both students and academics. Some Elements bridge the gaps between metaphysics, philosophy of science, and epistemology.

Cambridge Elements ≡

Metaphysics

Elements in the Series

Relations
John Heil

A full series listing is available at: www.cambridge.org/EMPH

Printed in the United States
by Baker & Taylor Publisher Services